HAMPSHIRE
Villages

Text by the Hampshire County Federation of Women's Institutes
Photographs by Ian Parker

COUNTRYSIDE BOOKS
Newbury, Berkshire

First published 2002
© Photographs – Ian Parker 2002
© Text – Hampshire County Federation of Women's Institutes 2002

COUNTRYSIDE BOOKS
3 Catherine Road
Newbury, Berkshire

To view our complete range of books,
please visit us at
www.countrysidebooks.co.uk

ISBN 1 85306 753 9

The front cover photograph shows Micheldever
and the back cover photograph shows Burley.
The photograph on page 1 is of Hambledon

Designed by Graham Whiteman

Typeset by Techniset Typesetters, Newton-le-Willows
Produced through MRM Associates Ltd., Reading
Printed in Italy

FOREWORD

This all-colour book is a celebration of some of Hampshire's most photogenic villages. Along with superb pictures by landscape photographer Ian Parker, it brings together many of the accounts of village life contained in *The New Hampshire Village Book*, first published in 1990.

Geographically, Hampshire is a large county edged by the sea, with the New Forest, historic cities and beautiful towns and villages. This book gives you the opportunity to see the diversity of this truly wonderful county, with its gentle rolling landscape.

So, please take the time to come and share with us Hampshire in all its glory. We are proud to welcome you to our beautiful county.

Jean Johnson
County Chairman
Hampshire County Federation of Women's Institutes
Autumn 2002

St Mary's church, Hartley Wintney

⌘ ABBOTTS ANN

Abbotts Ann lies in the north-west corner of Hampshire three miles south-west of Andover. It is picturesque with many thatched cottages and a peaceful trout stream flowing through water meadows. Originally known as Anna, the name Abbotts Ann was given to the village in AD 901, after King Edward the Elder granted 15 hides of land from the valley to the Abbey of St Peter at Winchester.

The most famous tradition in Abbotts Ann is the awarding of Virgins' Crowns, made to mark the death of men or women who were chaste in all senses, providing they were born in the village and were full members of the village church. The crowns were made of hazel twigs decorated with paper rosettes and had five parchment gauntlets hanging from them. At the funeral they were carried in front of the coffin by two girls dressed in white, and following the burial were hung above the font for three weeks to allow time for anyone to challenge the right of the deceased to this honour. The crown was then hung in the nave of the church, a small plaque being placed above with the dates of the Virgin's lifespan. The most recent crown was awarded in 1974.

In 1806 a young blacksmith named Robert Tasker came to live in the village. His invention of an improved plough in 1859 was such a success that he and his brothers built their own foundry in Anna Valley. During the Second World War, Taskers were famed for their long trailers – not least the 'Queen Mary', invaluable for transporting aeroplanes.

A delightful thatched cottage in Abbotts Ann

In the early 1930s, the Government bought Little Park Farm on the edge of the village and formed the Land Settlement Association. Families from the depressed areas of the North-East were settled, each being given ten acres, a bungalow and a pig. The produce was sold by a central co-operative. During the 1970s this system was no longer considered viable. Settlers were given the option of buying their holdings and the remaining land was bought by the Hampshire College of Agriculture.

⌘ AMPFIELD

Ampfield derives its name from the spring that still rises within the church's grounds. 'An-felde' was the village's earliest name, 'an' being a Celtic word for a spring.

On the site of Gosport Farm stood a pilgrims' inn called 'God's Port', drawing its business from the old Saxon road running between Romsey and Winchester, and drawing its water from the ancient spring at Washers Well. The route of the main road has changed, however, and now the busy A31 carries its traffic well away from the site of the old inn.

The Rev W. Awdry, author of the *Thomas the Tank Engine* books, lived as a small boy in Ampfield, where his father was vicar of St Mark's. His earliest recollection is of going down Pound Lane, climbing up the embankment, and strolling along the old London & South-West Railway line.

The two World Wars did not pass Ampfield by. During the First World War a 'holding camp' was established here for horses on their way to France, but one day 20 of them vanished into the bogs off Pound Lane when a noisy train caused them to bolt into the undergrowth. The same area was used as a decoy aerodrome during the Second World War, complete with lights and what looked like a control tower. The Old Thatches public house became a First Aid post and the White Horse a mortuary (though it was never used).

Until the 1930s Ampfield was a village predominantly feudal in character, dominated by the Ampfield House and estate, which comprised some 1,600 acres. In 1902 the Faber family took possession of the house and all the surrounding farms, and David Faber's death in 1931 led to the final break-up of the estate the following year. Today Hilliers, nurserymen, owns the house and some of its land.

⌘ ASHMANSWORTH

This small village in the north of the county stands on a high ridge very near the Berkshire boundary and has wonderful views of both counties. It is a long scattered village mostly devoted to agriculture and has at least five farms of some size. There is a pleasant mixture of old thatched cottages and Hampshire flint houses.

In the 10th century the ancient manor of Ashmansworth was granted to the

Church in Winchester for the maintenance of the monks there and it remained for the most part in church ownership until the beginning of the 19th century, when it passed to the family of the Earl of Carnarvon.

The 12th century church of St James has some medieval murals although only a small section of these are now visible. In the porch there is a 20th century engraved window 'In praise of music' in memory of the composer Gerald Finzi, who lived in the village for many years.

There is a modern, active village hall and the pub is popular with locals as well as long distance walkers on the Wayfarers Walk, which passes the edge of the village. In August the annual Flower Show and Fete attracts entries from all the neighbouring villages.

The war memorial on the green in Ashmansworth

⌘ ASHURST & COLBURY

Visitors to the New Forest who travel along the A35 from Southampton to Lyndhurst pass through Ashurst village. Some may discover it on a visit to the Longdown Activity Farm. Others come by train to the local station, 'Lyndhurst Road', or stay at the well-equipped Ashurst campsite. All are within the administrative area of the newly formed civil parish of Ashurst and Colbury (1986).

Originally there were four villages: Colbury, Foxhills, Longdown and Ashurst. The name 'Ashurst' does not go back beyond the 1920s; prior to that it was known simply as Lyndhurst Road from the adjacent railway station, built in 1847. As its name denotes, this station was intended to serve Lyndhurst residents, gentry staying at Lyndhurst hotels or country house parties. This was the nearest approach permitted by local landowners and the line was nicknamed 'The Weymouth Wanderer' from its circuitous route!

Colbury village centres round the church in Deerleap Lane and the Memorial Hall on Hunter's Hill. The name allegedly goes back to the 13th century when land was granted to the monks of Beaulieu Abbey to build a chapel at Colbury.

In 1870 Frank Ibbotson built the church at Colbury and endowed the living. He also built two schools at Colbury and Longdown. Marianne Vaudrey Barker-Mill, daughter of Frank Ibbotson, is a local legend. She built the Colbury Memorial Hall in 1928 in memory of her son Claude and other young men who died in the First

World War. She made her home in Colbury, building Langley Manor where she administered her estates with charity and charm. She initiated a clothing fund for her estate workers which she personally supervised, and her annual tea-party and fete was a social highlight.

⌘ AWBRIDGE

Awbridge's (prounounced Aybridge) main attraction is its lovely rolling countryside. The beech woods and rhododendron-lined roads are a delight in spring. One boundary follows the river Test and there are several trout lakes. The lake at Awbridge Danes was made in the 1920s to provide work for the local unemployed, each man receiving one shilling a day and a loaf of bread.

Roman occupation in the area is suggested by a villa found on aerial survey, and tiles, pottery and coins have been found at Awbridge House dating from AD 307. The Saxons, and later the Normans, had hunting lodges at nearby Stanbridge Earls (whose estates until recently covered large parts of the village) and Awbridge Danes, and the village is still well wooded.

For many centuries Awbridge was a very small settlement. By the 1600s there were only half a dozen substantial houses, of which four still stand. By 1800 there were about 40 houses and a population of some 400, and recent building has raised numbers further. Present inhabitants are mainly commuters to nearby large towns but there are still half a dozen farms, a mushroom farm, golf course, nurseries and smallholdings, builders and small engineering firms.

The parish itself is relatively modern, having been carved out of surrounding parishes in the 1870s. The church was built in 1876 at a cost of £2,800 and is a pleasant, unpretentious building in pretty surroundings. The village school dates from 1877.

⌘ BARTON-ON-SEA

Barton-on-Sea looks out to Christchurch Bay, with a frontage over a mile long. It has earned fame by giving its name to a type of fossil found in its cliffs and clay. In addition to fossils many palaeolithic implements have been found in the area, mainly around Chewton Bunny. There is a collection of these implements in the Ashmolean Museum in Oxford.

In the late 18th and early 19th centuries when smuggling was rife, Barton's cliffs, with their commanding views of Christchurch Bay and the Isle of Wight, provided excellent facilities for surveying the coast and making sure all was clear for a landing. Forest ponies were often used, with sacks on their backs to hold the kegs of brandy and other goods. Situated on the clifftop at the west end of Barton was Naish Farm. A tunnel ran from the farm to Chewton Glen (where the well known luxury hotel now stands).

During the First World War Barton Court Hotel, situated on the cliff top and now gradually slipping into the sea, became a convalescent home for British troops. Later, huts were erected along the cliff top of Barton Drive and hundreds of Indian troops were sent to convalesce there. An obelisk stands at the bottom of Barton Court Avenue to commemorate their stay.

Repeated falls have, over the years, reduced dramatically the area of the cliff top. The golf course at the eastern end of the cliffs had its origins in 1897 when a nine hole course was made on the cliff top. This was followed by an inland course in 1909 and the present course in 1932. Cliff erosion has presented problems here too and extra acres have been purchased at times. The erosion continues – so do the problems.

The novelist Elizabeth Goudge lived for a while with her parents in Barton Lane. In her autobiography she described Barton as 'a flat green plateau that is now a vast bungalow town'.

⌘ BASHLEY

The New Forest is to the north of the village, and the sea two miles to the south, past the now large urban area of New Milton and Barton-on-Sea.

The Danes had a great battle with the Saxons to the east of the village in the area called Wootton Rough, and the stream known as Danestream, that runs alongside, is said to have run red with blood. The housing to the south-east of the village is called Daneswood.

Road names come from inhabitants who used to live there, for instance Marks Lane from Mark Whitcher who lived in the corner cottage, formerly known as Mark's Cottage. Some roads are named by what went on there, eg Marlpit Lane – where marl was dug for the local handmade brickworks. At the corner of Smithy Lane and Bashley Cross Road there was a blacksmith's.

On the corner of New Lane and Bashley Cross Road are two cottages. The one known as 'Missioners' was a chapel. The one known as 'Taverners' was a wayside inn. The original village shop was part of the cottage known as 'homestead' by the smithy. It has two front doors – one of which was the shop door. It did a roaring trade whilst the railway line was being built in 1887 to 1888, selling goods to the Irish navvies.

The Football Club has gone from strength to strength in recent years. They use the recreation ground for matches and training and have built a clubhouse next to the village hall. There are also teams of youngsters who play regularly.

⌘ BASING

Basing is one of many small villages in the north-east corner of Hampshire. It has many traditional activities, such as the annual carnival. The lovely 11th century

The gardens of Basing House attract many tourists (taken by kind permission of Basing House)

church of St Mary has a flower festival, and a horticultural show attracts many exhibits in the village hall.

The ruins of Basing House are a great tourist attraction. It is said that the Marquis of Winchester held out in this house for two years during the Civil War, until it was stormed by Cromwell's army and captured in 1645. Also Queen Elizabeth I is believed to have visited Basing in 1601 and slept the night in the house.

The main roadway through Basing is named The Street. Today it is a busy thoroughfare, but going back to the 1930s this was a street where everything happened, but at a much slower pace. The ruins of Basing House at one end where children loved to explore the mysterious tunnels, and the peaceful river Loddon at the other where children often splashed about in the clear water.

The rows of cottages were homes for farm workers on the Hackwood estate. There was a forge which was manned by Richard Hall and his partner, Mr Wiggins, where the farmhorses came to be shod and the farming implements were repaired.

Bartons Mill and Lower Mill are on the banks of the river Loddon which flows through the village and these mills gave employment to a few, but most people walked or cycled into nearby Basingstoke to work.

If you are really lucky, you may see a ghost dressed in a long blue dress and dark cloak walking from the recreation ground along The Street and vanishing near the river Loddon. Yes, Basing is a lovely village to look at, and it also has an air of mystery!

⌘ BAUGHURST

Baughurst, pronounced Borg-hurst, is situated on the north Hampshire/Berkshire border in the middle of the Newbury/Basingstoke/Reading triangle. Baughurst means 'bog wood' and although there are still a number of gravel pits around the surrounding district to account for the excess water, the woods have long since been cleared for housing development.

Aldermaston Park became Aldermaston Aerodrome during the Second World War and was used by the Americans. Thereafter it became the Atomic Weapons Establishment employing a large number of people. To accommodate these people, large area of Baughurst and Tadley Commons were transformed into award-winning housing estates. Although many light industries have since moved into the area, AWE is still by far the main employer.

Baughurst Road is about four miles in length and the village can boast four public houses, a post office and a parade of shops. A derelict bus depot in Baughurst Road has recently been saved from demolition by developers when a local planning officer from Basingstoke & Deane Council noticed it had a unique feature. The timber-framed building had been built in the earlier part of the last century in a style favoured for a great many factories and warehouses, but featured the largest single-span roof in Western Europe – the roof trusses span some 80 ft from end to end without support underneath.

The present St Stephen's church was built in 1845 on the site of a Saxon church which has burned down. It is Gothic in style with an unusual octagonal tower. The church contains a 15th century choir screen which is rich in carving and is said to have been the gift of a Lord Chancellor of England, Archbishop Warham.

⌘ BEAULIEU

The Cistercian village of Beaulieu grew out of the abbey, founded by King John in 1204. Its mill, wells and High Street fascinate visitors as they walk on its uneven and ancient stones. The Beaulieu estate came into the possession of the Montagu family in Henry VIII's time.

Lord Montagu has opened his house to the public since 1952 and very much enjoys meeting his many visitors. Together with the Abbey and the Motor Museum, Beaulieu is well placed in the country's 'league' of stately homes. The

Palace House, home of the Montagu family since 1538

famous Montagu Motor Museum was founded in memory of his father, John Montagu, who successfully persuaded Parliament to abolish the 12 mph speed limit, and obliged motorists to register their cars and obtain licences to drive them. It was he who equipped the Army in India with mechanical transport during the First World War. Edward, the present Lord Montagu, is a vintage car enthusiast. Edward's mother, the Hon Mrs Pleydell-Bouverie, lived in the village from 1920 and was a founder member of the Beaulieu Women's Institute.

The village fire brigade was one of the earliest in the county of Hampshire, and before the Second World War was the private fire brigade of the Beaulieu estate. The village shops form the centre of village life and include an art gallery, a craft shop and Beaulieu Chocolates, whose hand-made chocolates are sold worldwide. The village hall hosts lectures, dramas, bingo, elections, weddings and many other events. A vineyard flourishes on the south facing slopes above the museum.

One could not leave Beaulieu without mentioning the river, with Bucklers Hard so near to the centre of the yachting world, together with the riverside farms, woods, bird sanctuary, and the estuary shores so abundant with wildlife.

⌘ BEAUWORTH

Beauworth lies on a sweep of high ground, the Millbarrows Ridge, on the northern side of the Hampshire downs in what has been designated an Area of Outstanding

Natural Beauty. Prehistoric long barrows are evidence of early occupation, and, according to charters dating from AD 909, its boundaries lay within the Saxon manor of Tichborne and the village was recorded in the Domesday Book. The earliest cottages, Church Terrace (once three but now two homes), date from the 16th century. In the early 1800s the centre room was used as a school room. A number of cottages are thatched and several had indoor wells.

The Saxon church has disappeared; the only remains are stone heads in Cheriton churchyard. The present church of St James was built in 1833 by Mr H. Mulcock, who owned a brick kiln at nearby Shorley Farm, in Cheriton, where local clay was used to make tiles, flower pots and extra-large bricks.

The earliest cottages in Beauworth date from the 16th century

One day in June 1833, some boys were playing near the village pond, now drained and forming part of the garden at Manor House Farm. One boy stumbled over what appeared to be a piece of lead pipe. His companions scrabbled in the ground with their fingers and discovered what they thought was an old metal box full of buttons. They hastily filled their pockets then ran home to tell their parents. The 'buttons' were in fact coins, about 6,000 in all and in mint condition, dating from the reigns of William the Conqueror and William II. They were declared treasure trove and are now in the British Museum. The lead coffer in which they were found is in Winchester Museum.

Another find was made in 1957 when, in an area of heavy undergrowth, Roman tiles and building materials were found. These led to the discovery of the site of a Roman villa covering some two and a half acres – further evidence that this has long been considered a desirable place to live.

⌘ BEDHAMPTON

Bedhampton is one mile from the town of Havant and, in spite of the growth of the village, retains an attractive look where it lies close to the foreshore of Langstone Harbour.

The manor appears to have existed as far back as the 9th century. It is now in the caring hands of a charitable trust set up in 1967. The manor house is an excellent environment for the elderly. Close to the manor is the 12th century church of St Thomas.

A turreted house named The Elms (18th century) was acquired by Sir John Theophilus Lee and a room within named the Waterloo Room. Sir John was a friend of the Duke of Wellington, who was reputed to have dined there, and the room has been beautifully restored in white and Wedgwood blue. The house is also owned by the Manor Trust.

At the old Mill House in 1819, John Keats the poet stayed with the master baker Mr John Snook and his wife. He had walked from Chichester for a house party, and this is where he finished his poem *The Eve of St Agnes*. He also spent his last night in England here when his ship was delayed in Portsmouth because of a storm. Subsequently he left for Naples, where he died in 1821.

Bedhampton had its share of smuggling in the past. Langstone Harbour was the haunt of smugglers during the 18th and 19th centuries and there was many a skirmish with the Revenue officers chasing after such men. A then nearby inn, the Cat and Fiddle on Bedhampton Hill, is said to have been used by them.

⌘ BENTLEY

Bentley is on the A31 between Farnham and Alton. It lies in the middle of an area which has been inhabited at least since Roman times and there are the foundations and floors of a Roman villa in a field at the western end. In the forest of Alice Holt is the site of one of the largest Roman potteries in the country.

In Norman and medieval times the houses clustered nearer to the 12th century church of St Mary which is on a hill about half a mile north of the main road. The Pilgrims' Way, which led by the shortest route from church to church from Winchester to Canterbury, passes through Jenkyn Place courtyard, where it is said the pilgrims used to stop and drink from a well called 'Jancknes's Well', from which the house gets its present name.

The church itself was much restored in the 14th and 15th centuries and again in the 19th. Jane Austen's brother Henry was perpetual curate of Bentley from 1824 to 1838 and lived at the 'old' rectory on the main road. With others in the parish he subscribed to the setting up of the cage, which was built for the 'temporary imprisonment of the drunk and disorderly'. Nothing of it now remains except the name, given to a row of cottages near the site.

The Eggar family have played a prominent part in the village and its surroundings since the 16th century and at one time owned Jenkyn Place and much of the surrounding land and properties. A Mr Sanderson, who was a director of the White Star Shipping Line, owners of the *Titanic*, was holding a dinner party at Jenkyn Place the evening he was told of the disaster in 1912.

Another famous Bentley resident was the Chief Scout, Lord Baden-Powell, who bought Blackacre in 1919 and changed its name to the world-renowned

'Pax Hill'. Since his death in 1941 the house has had various uses but is now a nursing home.

⌘ BISHOPS SUTTON

Should you be a passenger travelling on the Watercress Line steam train from New Alresford to Alton, the first village you will see from the right-hand side of the train is Bishops Sutton – or as written in the Domesday Book, 'Sudtone' meaning South Town. In 1136 King Stephen exchanged Sudtone with his half-brother Bishop Henry de Blois of Winchester for another manor in Surrey, hence it became Bishops Sutton.

Over the railway bridge you will see the 'faire great fermhowse' – Western Court – described by the surveyor of Edward IV in the 15th century as belonging to the Lord Chief Justice. It is now the home of the Coles family, who have in their possession a beautifully written account of two Beatings of the Bounds in 1745 and 1747, when men and boys of the village set up boundstones around the parish for Mrs Catherine Venables, lady of the manor Westerncourt. The boundaries, together with the names, ages and occupations of the 'beaters' are faithfully recorded – occupations such as coachbuilders, wheelwrights, blacksmith, carpenters, farmers, labourers, maltsters, woodmen, yeomen, servants, and an ex-'tythman'!

Next you will come to Sutton Manor, lying close by the 12th century church of St Nicholas. From the church you will see that the village runs alongside the cress beds where workers in their high, green rubber boots are tending the watercress in the streams, a major industry of the area.

The big garden of Whitefriars (formerly 'The Ruins') is where, in the mid to late 1800s, zebra, llamas, emu, peacocks and many other rare animals and exotic birds roamed free – for this was the great racing stables of Arthur Scotland Yates, the gentleman trainer who lived opposite Whitefriars in a large house called Lacklands. It was at these stables the fine horse *Cloisters* was trained, and you can imagine the excitement in the village when it won the Grand National of 1893. William Dollery was the winning jockey, and it is said that he built his house in the village named 'Cloisters' with his proceeds from that memorable race.

⌘ BISHOP'S WALTHAM

Bishop's Waltham is known as a small town but many still think of it as a village. Indeed it was winner of 'Southern England in Bloom 1998' in both Small Town and Best Kept Village categories. It is a nice place to live, but has known a hard life, when, to make ends meet, the women went stone picking, pea picking and strawberry picking.

There was a railway station but this has now gone to make way for a road across

Bishop's Waltham

the Pond. There were also two brickyards employing many local men. There are now two good council schools in the village, three churches and a Gospel hall, the Women's Institute, cricket and football teams and a youth club.

Bishop's Waltham House is a home for the frail built in ideal surroundings. The Priory was a seminary run by the White Fathers; after it was sold it became a police college. Cromwell knocked down the Bishop's Palace; the ruins still remain and are a great attraction. The Pond provided fish for the Palace but now the Fishing Club has taken over and fish themselves.

There are a number of footpaths where one can escape from the busy roads. The old railway track is now a public footpath, thanks to the Bishop's Waltham Society who worked hard to make this possible.

⌘ BLACKWATER

Situated in the north-east corner of Hampshire, Blackwater takes its name from the river which marks its boundary with the counties of Surrey and Berkshire.

In olden times a ford enabled people to cross the river easily, thus making the village an important changing stage for the coaches which ran along the main London to Exeter high road.

As well as two alehouses, there were three large coaching inns, of which one at least had its own brewery at the rear. While the horses were being rested or changed, the weary passengers could enjoy hospitality in the inns, heartened by the sight of rounds of beef, veal pies and hams, washed down with old port, burgundy or ale. Footpads and highwaymen abounded, making these journeys over the wild and desolate heathland, which surrounded Blackwater, extremely perilous. In 1839, 60 coaches a day were passing through the village.

Blackwater's greatest claim to fame must be its great two-day cattle fair. From the 13th century until after the First World War, it was held annually in November on the wide open spaces of commonland round the great crossroads to the south of the village. It was always mentioned in Old Moore's Almanac as the largest cattle fair in the south of England. Hundreds of cattle, horses, pigs and sheep were bought and sold.

The pine scented 'healthy' air attracted many people to settle here and gracious houses were built, each on its individual estate, with attractive lodges for the employees. More new villas and cottages housed the men who worked on the railway line which was laid in 1849, with a level crossing at the station in Blackwater.

Hawley Park is the oldest large house in the vicinity and has a chequered history. It was possibly a hunting lodge in the Middle Ages, then it was enlarged in the 18th century. There is, in the magnificent stable block, a clock dated 1743, still in perfect working order. These stables were used by Sir Francis Dashwood, the founder member of the notorious Hell Fire Club.

In 1860 Wilkie Collins, the author, stayed at Frogmore Park, another house in Blackwater. Did he see the ghost reputed to haunt it? It is said that his novel *The White Lady* was inspired by his visit there, others say he actually wrote the book during his visit.

⌘ BOTLEY

'Botley is the most delightful village in the world, it has everything in a village that I love, and none of the things I hate.' Thus wrote William Cobbett, author of *Rural Rides*, who farmed here for 13 years from 1805.

Vice Admiral Phillip Howard Colomb, who is buried in Botley churchyard, was not so well known. He introduced an important new worldwide system of signals and tactics upon the advent of steamships in the Navy in 1858. His work merits an entry in the Encylopaedia Britannica.

About 200 years ago the square was an area of turf and the market was held there. After a period of disuse the market was revived in 1830. On one occasion 1,280 sheep, 150 lambs, 250 cattle and 200 pigs were sold; each owner selling his own beasts. By tradition at the end of the market farmers sat down to a meal which always included Botley Plum Pudding.

The village grew around the square and it is said that there were 13 public

All Saints' church in Botley is just 150 years old

houses, so it is not difficult to imagine a grain of truth in the story that a man was hanged without judge or jury in the Catherine Wheel public house. This was later made a Temperance house and is now a bakery which still uses flour from Botley mill. During alterations the old wall revealed wattle and daub, which has been glassed over and is still on display.

Artefacts in the Manor Farm area show occupation from the Stone Age to Roman times on both sides of the river Hamble. This area is now the Upper Hamble Country Park, a Hampshire Recreational Centre, with a working farm, farmhouse, old barns, wheelwrights and forge.

All Saints' church is only 150 years old but the early Norman font which was dug up at Fairthorne was removed from the old church in 1835, as was the recumbent figure of John de Botteley.

⌘ BREAMORE

The present village of Breamore (pronounced Bremmer from its original Saxon name) lies along the busy B388 Salisbury/Ringwood road. The rosy brick cottages are mostly 17th century, built along the turnpike road by families whose descendants live locally to this day. Villagers worked on the Breamore House estate or leased farming land from the estate.

It is a pretty village with colourful gardens and flowering trees by the road, but life is made difficult for residents as the road cuts it in two. The school and shop lie on one side and the village hall and the Bat and Ball pub on the other. Seventeenth century stocks stand very near their original site opposite the pub. Villagers must have been fairly well behaved as records show the stocks were seldom used.

The original village of Breamore lay to the west of the road across the marsh, where people have grazing rights for geese and cattle and one is often held up while a procession of geese cross the road. It was centred round the Saxon church and is worth exploring to find old hidden cottages, and to take time to visit the church.

Here too is the gateway to Breamore House park. The house is an Elizabethan manor house built in 1583 by Queen Elizabeth's Treasurer, William Doddington. It stands in a splendid position on the hill slope, backed by sheltering woods and

Cattle and geese graze on Breamore's water meadow

looking out across a stretch of farmland and 17th century water meadows. The house is still a family home but is open to the public in the summer season. There is much to see – even a ghost, or two, if you are lucky (or unlucky).

You will not find any traces of the major battle that took place in the 5th century near the house but, if you walk up through the woods you come to the medieval maze, known as the Miz Maze.

⌘ BROCKENHURST

Brockenhurst, named in the Domesday Book as Broceste, is in the heart of the New Forest. Surrounded by everything rural, it is still within easy reach of Southampton, Winchester and Bournemouth, with a fast main line train service to London and a branch line to Lymington with connections to the ferry to the Isle of Wight.

It is said that it was an ancestor of Purkiss the grocer who discovered the body of William Rufus, after he had been killed in the Forest in 1100 by an arrow. In about the year 1087 Rufus had his horses shod and his armour, pikes and his arrow tips all made at the smithy which stood on the site of the present 'Island Shop'.

There are several churches including a Roman Catholic church completed in 1939 and St Nicholas', mentioned in the Domesday Book of 1086. In the churchyard is an old yew tree known to be at least 1,000 years old. Also in the churchyard is the grave of 'Brusher' Harry Mills who died in 1905. He was the local snake catcher and his gravestone was subscribed for by the people of the parish. One villager used to recall how her grandmother often met him whilst out walking in the Forest. 'Brusher' would be carrying his sack full of snakes, and he would say to her 'Put your hand in, Mother' – an offer she hastily declined!

In the summer the village is filled with visitors. Hollands Wood holds about 2,000 campers in caravans and tents, and there are very many delightful walks, ponds and streams in the area.

There are many attractive cottages, some of them thatched. One of the latter, Ash Cottage, once the home of Miss Bowden Smith, was the first village school and pupils paid 1d a week to attend. Shops, garages, hotels, guest houses and rest homes provide work for local people. There is also an engineering works and stables. One public house, the Rose and Crown, provided the village with its first

St Nicholas' church, Brockenhurst, is mentioned in the Domesday Book

bus service. Many of the villagers work at the Esso oil refinery at Fawley and other establishments connected with the oil industry.

⌘ BROOK & BRAMSHAW

Brook and Bramshaw are two villages situated just inside the New Forest. The villages have changed considerably over the last few years, with the M27 motorway just one and a half miles away. However, the area has certainly not lost its charm and the New Forest ponies still walk along the roads and graze the verges and commons. It is not only ponies that have to be avoided by passing motorists but cows, donkeys, pigs and occasionally deer.

There is still the old forge building in Bramshaw. This has a long history and the cottage adjoining is dated 1793, with the initials 'W.H.'. William Henbest placed an advertisement in the *Salisbury and Winchester Journal* on 1st September 1794, respectfully informing the public in general 'that he has erected a Foundery to cast iron of every sort'. In 1813 he made numerous cast iron safes for local churches at £3 13s 6d each. There is one in Salisbury Cathedral, embossed with the initials 'W.H.' and 'Bramshaw Foundery'.

Great attractions in the area are the two golf courses. One is over the open forest with spectacular views, but here the players have the added handicap of the ponies wandering on and off the greens. The main course is the venue for several tournaments, and the complex includes an hotel.

On the outskirts of Brook is the famous Rufus Stone. In August 1100 William Rufus, King William II of England, was shot dead by an arrow whilst he was out hunting in the Forest. The stone marks the spot where William Rufus died. Was it an accident, or was it murder by the hand of the French nobleman Walter Tyrell? The mystery remains to this day. Very near to the stone is the public house called the Sir Walter Tyrell.

⌘ BROUGHTON

Broughton has had a very long history, as proved by the discovery of the skeleton of a Saxon warrior, found on Broughton Hill by a ploughman in 1875. The blond hair only disintegrated on being exposed to the air. A 'pig' of Mendip lead, weighing 156 lbs and dated AD 59, the time of Nero, was found in 1783.

Henry V's soldiers, en route for the battle of Agincourt, encamped in a field near Bossington, part of the parish of Broughton.

As recently as 1829, the owner of Bossington House, a Mr Penleasze, destroyed the hamlet around, and a broadsheet published in 1870 laments this destruction, beginning thus: 'Alas poor Bossington. What is thy village fled? Where are thy natives gone? None left, but sleeping dead?' Before this event, Thomas South, also owner of Bossington House, and inventor, discovered that by covering a hot air balloon with a net, the difficulties of attaching a basket could easily be overcome. He also invented appliances for raising sunken vessels and keeping damaged ones afloat, and conducted experiments in the river Test.

In the 13th century, John Maunsel, lord of Broughton manor, was granted a charter by Henry III to hold an annual fair. Six hundred years later the reputation of the fair had sunk to 'a nasty mixture of beer and gingerbread'. In July 1871, the fair was discontinued. However, in modern times it has been resurrected and still the ale and gingerbread are present in the form of competition. A procession from the village hall stops at St Mary's church to obtain dispensation and renewal of the charter.

However, the ancient custom of carrying a man on a hurdle and depositing him on the doorstep of newcomers in the parish, when he would start brushing the step and refuse to go away until he had been given food and drink, has not been revived!

⌘ BURGHCLERE

Burghclere was for many centuries a prosperous farming area. Sheep and barley were the chief sources of income with their associated products, wool, meat and beer. In recent years the small mixed farms have mostly disappeared, but some dairy cattle, a few sheep and light riding horses can still be seen.

Ladle Hill is an Iron Age earthwork on the southern ridge, and far bigger is Beacon Hill on the western side of the road. These were human settlements 4,000 and 3,000 years ago. They later became look-out posts guarding the important route to the coast, then called the Salt Road, now the busy A34.

In the main village the chief centre of interest is the Sandham Memorial Chapel. It was built in memory of a soldier killed in the First World War, but its main claim to fame is the series of paintings executed by Stanley Spencer on its inner walls. The general effect of the work is macabre because the human figures are stiff and wooden but details are beautifully drawn. The scenes are from behind the Gallipoli war front.

Down in the south-east of the parish is Earlstone House. Its foundations are Norman but the present house dates from the time of James I. Also in the south-east is Watership Down, a pleasant hilltop with literary associations.

Most of the land in the area belongs to Lord Carnarvon, so the village feels it shares in the fame of the 5th Earl who, with Howard Carter, uncovered the wonderful treasure of Tutankhamen.

⌘ BURLEY

Standing on the edge of Cranesmoor and looking up towards the old smugglers' road, it is still possible to mistake sudden movements of a grey or brown forest mare amongst the heather, for the flash of Lovey Warne's petticoats as she ran to warn smugglers of the imminent arrival of the Excise men. At night she would hang a lantern in a tree near Picket Post as a warning, for Burley was the centre of the old smuggling trade.

The Queen's Head Inn is the oldest building in Burley, dating from the middle of the 17th century. The queen of the title could have been Elizabeth I, although no one knows for certain. In 1848 a village smithy and forge were mentioned as being part of the inn, a meeting place in those days for the smugglers planning their 'runs', over jugs of ale.

One hundred and fifty years of Burley history was celebrated in 1989, commemorating the anniversary of the church of St John the Baptist, while the chapel has celebrated over 200 years.

Thomas Eyre (1752–1829) was one of the better known names in the village, and there was old Mrs Evemy who lived to be over 100. The Herberts (family name of the Earls of Carnarvon) came to the 'Old House' in the mid 19th century, and Auberon lived in his beloved forest until he died in 1906. Another long-lived lady who died in 1981 in her 108th year was Constance Applebee, who pioneered women's hockey in America and who, on her 100th birthday received telegrams

Burley Manor

from the Queen and from the President of the USA. There is now a stained glass window dedicated to her memory in the church.

⌘ BURSLEDON

Early scribes were casual about spelling, and the place name was written variously as Brixenden, Burtlesden, Bristelden, Bussleton and Brixedone.

In 1154 Henry de Blois, Bishop of Winchester, allocated land to the French monks at Hamble, instructing them to build a church at Brixedona, 'to serve it well and maintain it'. By 1230 St Leonard's was completed. When in 1888 Barney Sutton was digging foundations for a new vestry, he uncovered a mass grave which contained the bones of large men thought to have been killed in battle. These were considered to have been the crew of one of the Danish longboats from a fleet defeated by King Alfred in AD 871.

Through the centuries ships were built at Bursledon, the first important launching being that of the man o'war *St George* in 1338. Henry V's *Grace Dieu*, whilst laid up, caught fire in 1439. Whether this was caused by accident or lightning is not known, but when a 'son et lumiere' was staged in the church in 1975 the producers took the opportunity to include a very realistic thunderstorm.

With bad roads, and no bridge until 1880, the river was the main highway, and sailing ships carrying cargo moored in the deep water off the Jolly Sailor. The railway came in 1888, blocking the top end of Badnam Creek which formerly gave access to Hungerford, where bolts were made for the wooden ships.

Mrs Shawe-Storey, who lived at 'Greyladyes' until her death in 1937, was responsible for the elaborate brickwork and chimneys around the estate. She also provided the richly decorated Roman Catholic chapel.

John Iremonger Eckless was a notable villager who lived at 'Upcott' from 1790 to 1869. He obtained pardons from William IV and George IV for agricultural labourers sentenced to transportation, and he was highly regarded by Lord Palmerston, who consulted him on such matters. He helped shipwrecked emigrants who were landed at Southampton, destitute, and obituaries in Hampshire newspapers testified to his great generosity and kindness.

⌘ CHANDLER'S FORD

In the early 1920s Chandler's Ford was a small village surrounded by beautiful woods and fields. The main road running through the centre, linking Southampton to Winchester, was quiet and traffic free. Now the village has grown in all directions and is a very busy place.

There were many groups of thatched cottages, interspersed with large properties set in several acres of land, and a number of market gardens and dairy farms. The springs and little streams have mostly been piped, converging where the railway station used to be, under the name of Monks Brook. The whole area was densely wooded, chiefly oak, yew and sweet chestnut. In the autumn lorries used to come to gather the fallen chestnuts to take to town for sale.

Before the railway works came to Eastleigh providing employment, the main industry was brick making. Bricks were taken from here by rail to London to build the Law Courts in the Strand.

In the 17th century, cherry trees grew in abundance throughout the village and each year people came from surrounding places to buy cherries (or merries as they were called). Oliver Cromwell's son Richard brought his wife from Hursley to enjoy the Merrifeasts.

During the Second World War, American troops were stationed in Chandler's Ford before D-Day. The men ate and slept with their vehicles which were parked under the trees along the roads. Many friendships were formed with local people and the children were given food they had never seen before – such as white bread, tinned peaches and tinned ham.

⌘ CHAWTON

Chawton lies in the valley of the river Wey, two miles from Alton. The village was

Jane Austen lived here in Chawton

known in Saxon times and was described in the Domesday Book as the manor of Celtone.

Chawton, being on the main pilgrim route to Winchester, had need of a coaching inn, which later became the house in which Jane Austen spent the last eight years of her life and where she wrote *Pride and Prejudice, Sense and Sensibility, Mansfield Park, Emma* and *Persuasion*. She lived here with her mother and sister Cassandra, who are both buried in Chawton churchyard. Jane, who died in 1817, is buried in Winchester Cathedral. Before being officially opened to the public in 1949, the house was used as a working men's club. It was bought by a Mr Carpenter and given to the Jane Austen Society in memory of his son.

Another interesting house is Clinkers, which was the village blacksmith and wheelwright's for about 400 years. The family were protected from evil by a mummified cat and rat in the roof – reputed to be good luck charms! Another house, Baigens, is possibly one of the oldest houses in Hampshire. Elizabethan murals were found behind the plastered walls. It also has a slightly sinister past, as a Mr Baigen was found hanging from a tree in what is now known as Baigen's Copse, north of the railway line near Chawton Park Woods.

The Knight family appear to have held land here since the reign of Edward II and purchased the manor in 1578. From that year there have been Knights at Chawton until the present time. The house is a beautiful example of Elizabethan architecture. Jane Austen's nephew Edward Knight, who was lord of the manor in the 19th century, established the first school in the village in 1840. This was for 'both sexes' and was established some 30 years before the Education Act of 1870 made schooling compulsory.

⌘ CHILBOLTON

Visitors to Chilbolton are intrigued to find a large 'Stars and Stripes', topped by a gilt eagle, adorning the village hall wall. A proclamation beside it declares that the citizens of Chilbolton have 'Honorary Citizenship of Montville, New Jersey'. What could they have done to have earned this honour? What connects this Test valley village with a town so far away?

The story began at the outbreak of the Second World War when Chilbolton was chosen as a suitable site for an airfield. In 1944, new craft were brought in, in preparation for the invasion of France. These were troop-carrying gliders, and the men who would use them were the 17th Airborne (US) paratroopers and glider-troopers. In December, in atrocious weather, they were towed into the air, the men inside crammed in like sardines, and crossed the Channel into France. There they took part in the 'Battle of the Bulge' in the Ardennes mountains.

In June 1984 a large contingent of ex-servicemen and their wives and families, numbering over 100, came to the village at the start of their 40th anniversary celebrations commemorating the D-Day landings. At the end of their visit, the

Chilbolton lies in the Test valley

veterans presented 'the citizens of Chilbolton' with an American flag, and a proclamation. The flag had been flown for a day from the Capitol in Washington in Chilbolton's honour, sponsored by the town of Montville, New Jersey (home of the 17th Airborne Division), and Honorary Citizenship of Montville bestowed on all citizens, in 'the interests of world peace'.

The flag now hangs in the village hall. An American lady, who had lived in the village some years previously, saw the flag during a return visit and on her return to the States, sent over a gilt eagle to top it. This trans Atlantic link is treasured by many in the village, and the striking emblem of the 17th Airborne has been incorporated into the Chilbolton panel of the Test Valley Tapestry.

⌘ COMPTON & SHAWFORD

As you can tell from its name, this is two villages in one. For the past hundred years it has been said, 'Compton is the one with the church and Shawford the one with the pub.'

There are traces of a Bronze Age settlement at Compton and parts of the Roman road still run through the village, whilst the busy Saxon road to the hamlet of Silkstead survives in the form of ancient tracks over the downs.

In 1836, whilst life in Compton continued to revolve round its fields and its Norman (previously Saxon) church of All Saints, the building of the Waterloo to Southampton railway was started and in 1882 a station was opened at Shawford. This resulted in the building of houses for the first commuters, who enjoyed the convenience of the railway and the beauty of district. The house agents' expression 'this favoured residential area', which is still used, dates back to this period. Thus the hamlet of Shawford became a bustling village with shops and an inn. This hamlet had previously consisted of a few cottages on the banks of the Itchen Navigation Canal and the great house of Shawford Park, built in the 17th century by Henry Mildmay.

The Navigation Canal was probably completed in 1729 and had been a busy commercial highway with a wharf near Shawford Mill and a regular passage of loaded barges, but with the coming of the railway the canal became a peaceful, reed-bordered waterway.

From this time Shawford continued as a residential area and at the turn of the 20th century more houses were built in fields at the top of the hill bordering the Roman road and separated from the village by Shawford Downs. Similarly, building was started on the top of the hill south of Compton village and separated from it by Compton Down. Between the two world wars these districts were particularly popular as residences for retired members of the armed services.

⌘ COPYTHORNE

Copythorne (meaning 'cropped thorn' from the practice of pollarding trees hereabouts) was a large common on the eastern edge of the New Forest. Now the parish consists of Bartley, Cadnam, Copythorne, Newbridge, Ower and Winsor.

Many road names relate to the past, such as Pollards Moor, Pound Lane, Barrow Hill and Whitemoor Lane (owing to the low-lying area attracting mist in the early morning and evening). Many Romany families settled here from the Forest where they had lived for generations and brought their trade names to the area, such as Wytcher (withy cutter for hurdles, pegs and baskets).

Half Moon Common is known as Bartley Regis, the royal connection dating from the time that a certain charcoal burner by the name of Purkiss came across the body of King William Rufus in a Forest clearing in 1100. In transporting the body to Winchester on his cart he rested at this spot.

Paulton's Park at Ower, the home of the Sloane Stanleys (owners of Sloane Square, London) since 1646, played a large part in the life of the community. The cricket club, which in 1989 celebrated their centenary year, started life in the celebrated Horseshoe Gardens, designed by Capability Brown, at Paulton's. They now have a portion of Copythorne Common as their permanent site, whilst Paulton's Park is now a well-known wildlife and leisure park, with an extensive rural life museum.

Before 1939, Johnson's Brakes used to come out from Southampton on a Sunday evening, bringing people to the 12th century inn, the Sir John Barleycorn, for a ride and a drink. Now the M27 whizzes traffic past to the west, and this beautiful thatched inn, reputedly the oldest in Hampshire, sits isolated, surrounded by the earthworks made by the building of the motorway. It is still popular with those who know of its existence and whereabouts.

⌘ CRONDALL

The Saxons called it Crundellan, which refers to the local Celtic chalk workings. This name, together with Crundelas and Crundale, justifies the insistence by many that Crondall should be pronounced 'Crundle'.

One's first impression is of a pleasing blend of houses of all ages, predominantly in mellow red brick. There are, in fact, 83 listed buildings in the village. Farmland entirely surrounds the compact community and imparts a rural atmosphere. As many tractors as men seem to be engaged in growing the crops of cereals, oil-seed rape, pulses, some maize and an occasional field of beautiful blue linseed. There are sheep, but now no hops are grown, neither are there dairy herds nor pigs. In the past there were spring-fed watercress beds, basket making, weaving, a malthouse – even tobacco growing, and an area of good clay gave rise to a brick industry. Nowadays the soils, whether clay or chalky loam, blessed with a high water table, make fertile ground for many lovely gardens. On occasions some of these are opened to the public. There is much riding and keeping of horses, and walkers enjoy an abundance of footpaths, which are ritually trodden on Rogation Sunday.

The Grade 1 listed Norman church of All Saints dates from 1170. It superseded a wooden Saxon building from which there only remains a fine stone font, still in use today. On view also is a small marble font, which a Puritan vicar had made to supplant the Saxon object 'profaned by Papal usage'. The present calm, uncluttered interior belies the vicissitudes of fashions and values. Parliamentary troops were actually quartered within the church during the Civil War, when skirmishes occurred in and around the village between Roundheads from Farnham Castle and Royalists from Old Basing and Alton. Fortunately no harm came to the famous brass of Nicholas de Caerwent, a 14th century rector. This is decorated with fylfot crosses, better known to us as swastikas.

On display is one of the country's few remaining 'pitch-pipes'. It was purchased in 1783 to aid the musicians who led the first singing of psalms and hymns. Curiously, it was the Church which bought the village hand-driven fire-engine in 1776, kept it at the back of the church for years and maintained it for a century or so. With leather pipes and buckets, it was still relied upon as the sole appliance in 1935! Now it has to be brought from its lodging in the museum in Winchester to be admired on very special occasions.

Detail on a house in Dippenhall Street, Crondall

⌘ CRUX EASTON

The hamlet of Crux Easton appears in records as far back as the 11th century as Estune. Then it became Eston Croc when it was given by William the Conqueror to Croch the huntsman (warden of Chute forest), from whom the present name probably derives.

A church is recorded in the Domesday Book. A Norman church, standing in the 12th century, was replaced by the present St Michael's in 1775 and restored in 1894, when a commemorative tree was planted at the crossroads.

The wind pump is said to be unique, being the only one of its kind remaining in Hampshire, if not the whole of southern England. It was certainly in use at the beginning of the 20th century, pumping water into a reservoir opposite where the Porchester estate cottages now stand, supplying only the present manor house. The original blueprints for this still survive.

In about 1692 Edward Lisle bought the estate and made copious notes of agricultural practices in the district. After his death his son Thomas, then rector of Burghclere, published these as the best-selling *Observations in Husbandry*. Edward Lisle had 20 children and his daughters built a grotto in what is now called Grotto Copse.

In 1897 when the Rev Charles de Havilland took the living, the village consisted of the rectory, church, school, farmhouse, pub and a dozen cottages. His son Geoffrey, who 'tinkered' with machinery, installed the first electricity into the rectory. Since the Rev de Havilland's day the village has changed. The village policeman left in 1930, the school closed in 1945, the pub in 1950 and the generations of rural families who lived in the cottages have gone, but their names live on in the names of the properties – Faithfulls, The Alders, de Havillands, Three Legged Cross.

⌘ DENVILLES & WARBLINGTON

Warblington Castle and the church of St Thomas à Becket have long been historical landmarks overlooking Emsworth harbour.

The then moated castle was destroyed by Parliamentarian forces during the Civil War in 1642 leaving only the tower and one side of the gatehouse. Warblington church (13th century) was at one time in the centre of a village which was wiped out by the Black Death. The houses fell into dereliction leaving only the church. The church has a partly Saxon tower and a fine 15th century timbered porch. Standing in the churchyard is a grand old yew tree which is reputed to be at least 1,500 years old. At the west and eastern ends of the churchyard are huts built to accommodate watchmen who were employed to prevent 'body snatching' when medical men, mainly students, desperate for cadavers on which to practise their profession, were willing to pay for a dead body.

Prior to the Second World War, Warblington House stood in its own grounds bordering Pook Lane and was occupied by the Marquis of Tavistock. Within the estate, enclosed by high brick walls, was a small wildlife park kept by the Marquis, specialising in parrots. The secretary to the Marquis was none other

Warblington castle seen from the churchyard

than the notorious traitor, William Joyce, who, having absconded to Germany, regularly broadcast enemy propaganda as Lord Haw Haw.

Denvilles, by comparison, is more recent development. In all probability the first houses were constructed in the late 19th century, the residents being mainly naval officers and businessmen.

⌘ EAST BOLDRE

Along the main road between Beaulieu and Lymington, lies the well known beauty spot of Hatchet Pond. This serene stretch of water reflects pine trees and is often marbled at sunset with pink, gold and the blood-red of a dying day.

When tired of idling here, take the turning sign-posted 'East Boldre'. The village is a long straggling one – a rural ribbon development, and the road leads eventually to East End, South Baddesley and the Lymington to Yarmouth ferry. Most of the houses are built on the left hand side of the lane, with open forest and grazing animals on the right.

Further on is the old schoolhouse and the village school which are situated on the right, between clumps of pines trees. The school was built in 1842, on four and a half acres of land presented by the young Queen Victoria, together with money from the Crown and the Church of England. The log books of these early times bear witness to the strict discipline enforced by the use of the cane for such offences as untidy arithmetic, loitering outside the school, kicking a dog, and having dirty boots!

This, the smallest and oldest school in the Forest, was a sad loss when it was closed in 1985, but there was one happy outcome. When closure was first mooted because of falling numbers, a sub-committee of the Parish Council was formed and, after valiant fund-raising efforts, the playing field and infants classroom were purchased for the modest sum of £9,000. This amenity is now used by the Scouts, Beavers and Cubs, the under-16s football club, and the Mothers and Toddlers Club, not to mention the annual church fete and countless other activities.

⌘ EAST MEON

East Meon is a picturesque village, four miles west of Petersfield. There have been Bronze Age finds near Westbury House, and Old Winchester Hill, now a nature

East Meon

reserve with extensive views over the countryside, was originally an Iron Age fort.

All Saints' church was built between 1075 and 1150 by Bishop Walkelin, who also organised the building of Winchester Cathedral. It is magnificently situated at the base of steeply rising, green Park Hill, overlooking the village. The most famous feature is a black marble font, from Tournai in Belgium, carved about 1150, depicting the Garden of Eden.

The river Meon rises behind South Farm and wends its shallow way through the village. During past centuries flooding of the river became a worsening problem, with streets and houses annually under several feet of water, even preventing children attending school. As there was no mains drainage or piped water, this brought additional problems from privies. In 1955 the course of the river was changed and widened. It now flows over a concrete base with many small bridges.

There are two lovely Tudor houses in Workhouse Lane (where there was a workhouse between 1727 and 1910) and several Georgian and earlier houses and cottages in the village centre. The Court House, now a private residence, has a large medieval barn from the same date. This was used by the Bishops of Winchester for the local manorial court and residence for the visiting bishop. It has 5 ft thick flint and stone walls, which are 50 ft high.

To the south of the village HMS Mercury – a naval communications school – occupies a sprawl of buildings over the hilltop by Leydene House. This magnificent mansion was the home of Eleanor Countess Peel, who, with her politician husband, built it in 1924, probably the last 'stately home' to be built in England. When Lady Peel died in 1949, the Navy bought the house and some of the land.

⌘ EAST TYTHERLEY

If you drive from Lockerley to West Tytherley, you will pass through one of the smallest villages in Hampshire – East Tytherley.

In 1335 Tytherley was given to Queen Philippa by her husband, Edward III. She loved the peaceful village, and when the appalling Black Death spread to London, she brought her court here for safety. Tragically, two of the young courtiers had already been touched with death's finger, and within a few days 70 per cent of the village died. Flemish weavers, who had been given sanctuary by the Queen from persecution in their own country, helped prepare the shrouds. Philippa created a semi-permanent court here, and names such as Queenwood and Queen's Croft remain.

After the Civil War, the Rolle family became lords of the manor and until 1800 lived in the village. Each generation added something to the history of the place. In 1736 Miss Sarah Rolle founded a charitable school, which exists to this day, and the beautiful old trees in the churchyard of St Peter's were planted by Dennis Rolle. Built in 1250, the church remained unaltered until 1863 when a porch and bell-tower were added.

The gatehouse to the manor, East Tytherley

Of course, East Tytherley has had its share of eccentrics. Sir Robert Peel's uncle, General Jonathan Yates, became tenant of the manor house, and was much admired by the village in spite of rather dubious morals. Amongst his hobbies was cock-fighting, and in the grand salon of the manor, turf was laid instead of carpet for matches between his birds and those of other landowners.

In 1849, a Mr Cooke bought half the estate, and while staying at Tytherley invented the electric telegraph. Telegraph Hill and Telegraph House are reminders of those times.

Today, the village is as peaceful and happy as it has ever been, though of course the cricket pitch sees some good battles, and the skittle alley in the Star Inn is a popular rendezvous.

⌘ ENHAM ALAMEIN

Enham was a tiny hamlet at the turn of the 20th century. Enham Place was a large house owned by Lord and Lady Earle, and there were two smaller houses, Littlecote and the White House, each with a few servants. Some villagers lived in their place of employment, others in lovely thatched cottages, or chalk and flint cottages with tiled roofs dotted along the Newbury to Andover Road which ran through the grounds of Enham Place.

In 1919 a consortium of London businessmen purchased Enham Place and started a rehabilitation centre for disabled men from the First World War. In 1939 Enham Place was demolished, and in its place Enham Industries was built, thus enabling victims of the war to help in the manufacture of Nissen huts and barrage balloons. Over the years several houses have been donated to the village by outsiders who have appreciated the work being done by the Enham Village Centre.

In 1942, after the battle of El Alamein, one of the turning points of the Second World War, some prominent Egyptians gave £100,000 to the Enham Village Centre as a mark of their gratitude to the men who had saved Egypt from occupation. It was then decided to rename the village Enham-Alamein. Plans were made to build 100 cottages, a hostel for the disabled, a church, a school and an inn. The houses were to be specially adapted for disabled personnel. The school and inn did not materialise, however, there being an excellent school in nearby Smannell.

Every year on Alamein Sunday in October, the young men of 1942 who turned the tide at the battle of El Alamein are remembered with a parade and service at St George's chapel.

Enham Industries has now diversified its products. Engineering, furniture making, book-binding, candle-making and wax items, electronics and horticulture give work for over 300 disabled men and women.

⌘ EVERSLEY & BRAMSHILL

Eversley has always been a forest parish of scattered hamlets. Long ago it was mostly heathland and pasture woodland like the New Forest. Later it had its own self-sown pine woods and now there are Forestry Commission plantations where many people enjoy walking and horse riding. There is pasture beside the Blackwater, which flows through Eversley and Bramshill and forms the county boundary with Berkshire. At nearby Eversley Cross, cricket has been played on the green for over 200 years.

Charles Kingsley was rector of Eversley from 1844 to 1875. It was here in the Old Rectory that he wrote *The Water Babies*. It is now a private house, but its appearance is little changed since the Kingsley family lived there. Charles and his wife are buried in the churchyard, their grave marked by a white marble cross with a passionflower entwined on it. Below their names and almost hidden in the grass are the Latin words 'Amavimus, Amamus, Amabimus', meaning 'We loved, We love, We shall love'. Charles Kingsley planted the avenue of Irish yews leading from the lychgate and the big Wellingtonia grew from a cone which he brought back from America and which his daughter planted a few days after his death. In the church is the pulpit from which he preached, now reduced from its former three-decker height. The church is the only one in Hampshire with an 18th century screen.

Bramshill is closely linked with Eversley. Its name means 'broom-covered hill' and Bramshill House stands on the hill with splendid views. It is now the Police Staff College and therefore not open to the public. It is a beautiful Jacobean house built by Lord Zouche between 1605 and 1612.

⌘ EWSHOT

Ewshot is small and consists of five hamlets: Ewshot Village, Beacon Hill, Warren Corner, Doras Green, and the new complex, known as Ewshot Heights, built by the late Charles Church. The postal address is Farnham, Surrey, the post code is based on Guildford, the telephone is via Aldershot, rates are paid to Fleet in Hart District, and the County Council is Hampshire at Winchester!

Many of the older houses were built with bricks made at the local brickworks, which no longer exists. Bricks were also supplied for the building of Ewshot Camp in 1900. Gravel from the local pits was used, much of which was transported on tramlines laid for that purpose, down the hill and through the woods and across fields. Sand too was required, and Sand Pit Cottages in Tadpole Lane mark an area where much sand was extracted.

The camp, when finished, was occupied by the Royal Artillery, and for many years the horses being exercised were a familiar sight in the village lanes. When Aldershot Camp was built in the 19th century, land known as Bourley Bottom became a catchment area. Five reservoirs were dug and water from the surrounding hills ran into them and was piped to form the water supply for the camp. It still does so today. The water bailiff's house is on the far side from Ewshot and in days past, the Ewshot postman had a long and bumpy ride across the common to take letters.

In the early 1920s, a local man started a bus service to Farnham, three miles away. If the passengers were lucky they rode all the way, but alas, they often had to get out and walk up the steep hills, as the bus couldn't make it when loaded. Later the Aldershot Traction Company took over.

⌘ EXBURY

Exbury must surely enjoy one of the most favoured situations in Hampshire, being on the edge of the New Forest, just one mile from the Solent coast and having its fields and woods overlooking the Beaulieu river. Its fortunes have been much tied up with the owners of Exbury House, a fine neo-Georgian mansion which stands in Exbury Gardens, now famous for their collection of azaleas and rhododendrons. In the 18th century Exbury House was owned by the Mitford family. The next owner was Lord Forster who, in 1919, sold the estate to Mr Lionel de Rothschild, whose son, Mr Edmund de Rothschild owns it today.

All the cottages in Exbury village were built for workers on the estate. The earlier ones are built of distinctive yellow bricks made at a brick kiln on the estate. Later when the gardens and greenhouses were being established, a large army of labourers and gardeners was recruited and houses were built for them in the 1920s in red brick. Mr de Rothschild also built an attractive bow-fronted shop and post office and a village club.

Exbury church was built in the early 19th century using some of the stones from a monastic chapel which had existed at Lower Exbury. Several members of the Mitford family are buried in the churchyard.

The most impressive monument is the Forster memorial bronze in the Memorial Chapel. It depicts Alfred Forster, son of Lord Forster who died of wounds sustained at the end of the First World War. A young sculptor, Cecil Thomas, was wounded at about the same time and for four months the two young men were in the same hospital and became great friends. After the war, Lord and Lady Forster commissioned Cecil Thomas to design a memorial to Alfred and his elder brother, John, who also died in the First World War. The bronze was so impressive that it was exhibited at the Royal Academy in 1924.

⌘ FAIR OAK & HORTON HEATH

'The old order changeth yielding place to new' – Tennyson's words are an apt comment on the parish of Fair Oak and Horton Heath. Once a small cluster of cottages, it has developed into a village with a population of around 8,000.

For many years the parish was known just as Fair Oak, the name of Horton Heath being incorporated in 1983. The name derived from the fair that was held near the oak tree in the square on 9th June every year. The fair was discontinued after the First World War and all that remains of the original oak tree is a chair made from its wood in Winchester Cathedral. A carving depicting it outside the George Inn is incorporated in panelling above a fireplace at Fair Oak Lodge in Allington Lane. The present tree was planted in 1843.

Inevitably, the surge in population has resulted in all sorts of changes, especially in amenities. The parish church of St Thomas has been extended. The church school was superseded by a large school campus on another site, with the original site now being used for sheltered accommodation for the elderly. When the church graveyard became full, a new cemetery was opened in 1942 and Mr Jesse Latimer was appointed gravedigger. Sadly, he died before he could start work and was accorded the dubious privilege of being the first person to be buried there. The latest amenity is a new village hall which serves a growing number of clubs and activities.

William Cobbett could never have foreseen the spoliation of this area on his frequent journeys between Winchester and Botley along what was then known as Cobbett's Road, but is now plain Winchester Road. He wrote of this route in his *Rural Rides* of 1832; 'a more beautiful ten miles there is not in all England'. Yet some of that beauty still survives in what is so unromantically known as the Green Belt, and human habitation has not quite driven out the wildlife. The village has its own designated nature reserve, Knowle Hill, adjoining the deer farm. Administered by the Parish Council it was once part of a rubbish tip.

⌘ FARRINGDON

Farringdon is a small village in the fold of the Downs between Selborne and Chawton. In his journal dated 13th February 1774, the naturalist Gilbert White mentions 'Great flocks of buntings in the fields towards Farringdon'. At the time he was curate of the 12th century church of All Saints at Farringdon as well as curate at Selborne. There are still many beautiful thatched cottages which Gilbert White must have seen on his rambles round the village and certainly the present yews in the churchyard were already old by that time.

Later, about 1877, the eccentric rector Rev Massey bought an old boarding school opposite the church and, with only the help of one bricklayer and his labourer, proceeded to add a tower and a wing and gradually covered the building with red brick, ornamented with beautiful terracotta work of pomegranates and other fruits. Work went on for the next 20 years and when the puzzled villagers pressed the rector for an explanation for what use he intended the building he would tease them by saying confidentially: 'I believe I shall make a tea house out of it. Do you know of a secondhand revolving light for sale, such as they use in lighthouses? I want one. When it turns green it would be tea time!' 'Massey's Folly', as it is now called, was divided into the school and village hall. Sadly the school closed in 1988, but the hall is still used by village organisations.

An unsolved mystery in 1785 is recorded in the churchyard where the tomb of Mary Windebank, aged 75, appears to tell of a murder in what is now Gilbert's Cottage. The top part of the stone is carved. It shows the old lady in a large fourposter bed, with a row of moneybags underneath. A thief is seen coming up the stairs and behind him is a curious winged figure thought to portray the Devil.

Simon Windebank married Mary in 1700. When he died he was quite well to do. The heir to the property was a certain John Heath. A stipulation in Simon's will stated that his widow was to be provided for and so, following the usual practice of the time, Heath mortgaged her house and its grounds. Mary's death is recorded in the burial register with no mention of murder. It is speculated that perhaps John came up the stairs simply to take charge of his own money and explain the new arrangements about the mortgage. But who put up the tombstone? Was it indignant Windebank relatives? John Heath lived comfortably in Farringdon until his death and the mystery was never explained.

Nationwide interest has been sparked by the discovery of a 14th century 'Doom and Last Judgement' wall painting in the church, dated about 1380, with another dated about 1400 painted on top, no doubt when a new patron commissioned it. It is the older of the two that is causing the most excitement, the blue pigment of the Saviour's robe making it a rare and very special find.

⌘ FORDINGBRIDGE

Fordingbridge sits on the edge of the beautiful New Forest, and its outstanding feature must be the river Avon, one of the best fishing rivers in the country. Salmon, trout, pike, chub and other coarse fish are plentiful and record catches have been recorded. The river flows alongside the recreation ground (as well as meandering round the houses) making this area a very pleasant place to wander. The old medieval bridge has seven arches and the centre one is 14 ft 6 inches wide, possibly constructed about 1362.

From 1870 until the First World War, a regatta was held each year. The boats and riverside gardens were illuminated, trainloads of people came down from London to 'Hampshire's Henley' and much fun was had by all.

During the Second World War the 3rd Royal Tank Regiment was stationed in and around Fordingbridge and from here dashed to Calais to cover the retreat from Dunkirk. Under the threat of invasion, the Royal Engineers were asked to drill into the foundations of the bridge to place charges of explosive so the bridge could be blown up if necessary. The men found it extremely difficult to drill into the stonework placed there in the 14th century. Later, during the war, the 7th corps of the US Army were just outside Fordingbridge and General Patton stood outside Locks, the chemist, watching his troops march through.

In the 14th century St Mary's was a very important church, Fordingbridge being the head of the Deanery which included Ringwood, Christchurch and the Forest parishes. It is very important to its parishioners today and the building itself is beautiful and such a peaceful place to worship.

⌘ FOUR MARKS

Four Marks is a unique self-made village, the result of the hard work and enterprise of its inhabitants. In the late 19th century it was merely a name on the map to mark the place where the four parishes of Farringdon, Chawton, Medstead and Ropley met. As this was an important beacon site in the Napoleonic Wars and all four parishes claimed it, the Bishop of Winchester decided to make it a special extra-parochial area bounded by four stone marks. In Telegraph Lane, near the highest point in Four Marks, there is a house called Semaphore Farm.

From then on Four Marks grew and established itself as a village. It was on the main stagecoach route from London to Winchester and Southampton, so

Fordingbridge is situated in the beautiful New Forest

development started on this road (now the A31). A garage was built by an enterprising mechanic and is now Chawton End Garage, run by his sons and grandsons.

Many people settled here after the First World War, building colonial-style bungalows with large gardens where they could grow vegetables or keep poultry to be self-supporting. By 1930 the population had increased to such an extent that in 1932 a council was duly elected and the first Parish Council meeting was held. A new church was built in 1956.

Two things were still needed to complete the village amenities – a burial ground and a recreation ground, and both of these were made possible by the purchase of two and a half acres of land. The generous bequest of a local nurseryman made it possible to buy more ground and establish a sports centre.

On the top of Swelling Hill there is a pond which, when Four Marks had no mains water supply, was a great standby in times of drought. But it fell into disuse and became so overgrown that it was little more than a swamp. In 1974 a team of enthusiastic helpers was formed and they dredged the pond, cleared the surrounding jungle, planted shrubs and plants, put up seats and even a wishing well. So hard did they work that they won the Daily Telegraph National Award for the best rehabilitated pond!

⌘ FRITHAM

In the north of the New Forest, a stone's throw from the Wiltshire border, nestles the ancient village of Fritham, a hamlet of less than 200 people, and mentioned in the Domesday Book as Thorougham or Truham. For generations this Hampshire village slept happily at the end of a track which dwindled into the silent forest. Most farmsteads had a few cows, pigs and hens and an acre or two which supplied their needs, and villagers teamed up and helped each other with the harvesting at the end of the year.

The village shop with its clanging door bell and indescribable smell of freshly baked bread, shoe polish and smoked bacon, was the main shopping centre and post office, and as the towns of Ringwood and Lyndhurst were a fair old pony and trap ride away they were not journeys to be undertaken lightly.

At the top of the lane, the banks of which are still dotted with primroses and bluebells in spring, stood the Royal Oak, one of the oldest pubs in the forest. It was renowned for its beer from the barrel, drunk in the little front parlour, often in the company of a pony or cow's head peering in through the open door, and to the accompaniment of the grunting pigs in the adjoining sty.

The other main meeting point in Fritham was the little tin chapel where services held twice on Sundays were attended by everybody in the village. Every child, willing or reluctant, was washed and scrubbed for the weekly visit to the Sunday school in the hut beside the chapel, which served as the junior school during the week and meeting place for the Band of Hope, sewing circle and socials most evenings.

Many of the old cottages had Forest Rights, which entitled the owners or tenants to collect wood and turf, and to pasture their cattle, ponies and donkeys on the forest. Pannage rights also allowed pigs to forage and root for acorns from 25th September to 22nd November, thus preventing the ponies from eating too many, a practice which is too often fatal. These rights belong to the chimney and hearthstone of the cottage, not to an individual, and several cottages in Fritham still hold on to them.

When the Schultz Gunpowder factory was built in an isolated glade by Eyeworth lake, life for the village changed overnight. The factory, making ammunition for sporting guns, provided work for most of the men and many women in Fritham and surrounding areas. The grass tracks, unchanged for decades, were strengthened with gravel from the forest, and huge carts drawn by teams of heavy horses trundled along the once deserted lanes. The tin chapel was 'adopted' by the factory owners, and a handsome brick building was erected. The village had never been so prosperous.

In 1912 disaster hit this tiny hamlet when five of its young men perished in the *Titanic* and, when the factory closed a few years later, Fritham returned to its sleepy isolated existence. Today, although much is unchanged deep in the glades and marshlands, and animals still graze the green and wander down the lanes, life in Fritham has changed considerably.

The shop and post office closed a few years ago, the Royal Oak has never been busier, but the little chapel holds only two services a month for a handful of people and sits silent and withdrawn, remembering perhaps the days when its congregation spilled out on to the forest.

⌘ GRATELEY

Grateley is situated in the north-west corner of Hampshire; the nearest town, Andover, is seven miles away. Grateley gets its name from the great lea or meadow, which lies to the south-west of the church. The church of St Leonard was built mainly in the 13th century, although some parts are said to be Saxon and three courses of bricks in the tower are thought to be Norman. The stained glass in the south window came from Salisbury Cathedral.

Grateley is a small village split into two parts. One part is made up of houses clustered around the church, Manor Farm and the Plough Inn. The other part is about a mile away and has developed since the railway line was built in the late 19th century, which attracted trades and businesses connected with coal and grain. The road joining the two ends of the village, known as Station Road, was once a private road which connected Grateley House (which belonged to the Boutcher family) to the station. The family did not wish to have a station near to the house, so it was built a mile away. The public house, once known as the Railway Hotel but now called the Shire Horse, was also owned by the Boutcher family until it was sold to the Gibbs Mew brewery.

There are general stores at both ends of the village and there is a local bus service to Andover. The station is just a halt now, but mainline express trains between London and Exeter still stop there.

⌘ GREYWELL

Greywell is a small village lying in the north-east of the county. The first Lord Dorchester (first Governor General of Canada) acquired the manor in 1786 and it has remained with the family ever since. It is alleged that the old manor house was on the east side of The Street where there is an extensive unexcavated mound of earth, perhaps the remains of the house.

The restored Basingstoke Canal, opened in 1798, ends in a tunnel, three quarters of a mile long, which in 1932 caved in at three places. It is now famous for one of the largest colonies of bats in the United Kingdom. Controversy reigns between the Canal Society, who would like to rebuild the tunnel and make it navigable and the naturalists who wish to preserve the bat colony. The river Whitewater rises and runs through the village and has the unique feature of passing under the canal. One bridge over the Whitewater is known as Tolls Bridge – Tolls being a former owner of the manor. Greywell is rich in wildlife, particularly wild flowers, and 15 acres of The Fen have been purchased by the Hants & Isle of Wight Naturalists' Trust to be managed as a nature reserve.

The church of St Mary the Virgin was built in the 12th century and on the Norman doorway the marks of the Crusaders' crosses can still be seen. The village hall celebrated its centenary in 1985 and is still in constant use for meetings, sales and playgroups, etc. Displayed in the hall are the stumps used in a cricket match on 8th, 9th and 10th September 1862 when Greywell played the England team – but sadly lost!

During the Civil War the whole area saw much activity and to this day there is a block of cottages known as The Barracks. Few changes have been made to the village, although the ditch along The Street to which housewives would cross the road to throw their slops has been paved over!

⌘ HALE

Few places can claim to have witnessed the 'seizing' of their village green, but such was the ritual performed on a bright Saturday afternoon in February 1975 in the presence of some 200 villagers.

Hatchett Green, as it is known, is one of the main attractions of the small village of Hale, which lies in the northern corner of Hampshire. The picturesque green, surrounded by fields, houses, the village school and the village hall, extends to about 13 acres.

The Hale Cricket Club has used it for many years and some exciting matches have been played on it, much to the delight of local spectators, who sit around the green every Saturday afternoon during the summer months.

For many years, in the absence of any indication of a legal owner or title to the land, Hale Parish Council had exercised a form of guardianship over the green. This ensured a degree of protection, but not being the owners of the land, the Council were unable to enforce their edicts. They therefore gave formal notice of their intention to 'seize' Hatchett Green and to hold it in perpetuity for the benefit of the inhabitants.

No-one came forward to oppose the 'seizing', but it was considered advisable to enact an ancient ceremony by which a person who had entered into possession of unclaimed land made it clear to his neighbours that he was the legal owner.

So, on 22nd February 1975, the villagers assembled on the green to see the ritual performed. The chairman of the Parish Council cut a sod from the green, held it up at arm's length, replaced it and solemnly proclaimed that the land was now vested in the parish. Registration of the Council's 'possessory title' at the Land Registry followed. An historic day for the village of Hale.

⌘ HAMBLEDON

Hambledon lies in a dry chalk valley just off the A3 road between Petersfield and Portsmouth. The area has been inhabited from earliest times, as there are traces of Iron Age barrows and worked flints have been found.

The first recorded royal visitor came to Hambledon in 1651. After defeat at the battle of Worcester, Prince Charles Stuart escaped. On his way to the coast, Colonel Gunter offered the future Charles II shelter with his sister, Ursula Symons, who lived on the outskirts of the village. It was a risky business as Hambledon was for Parliament. The house still stands and is known as 'King's Rest'.

Probably the great thing that Hambledon has been known for in more recent times is cricket. It was not

Camms Lane, Hambledon

invented here as some people think, but the rules of the modern game were standardised by the Hambledon Cricket Club. They played on Broadhalfpenny Down with a curved bat and two stumps. Hambledon's finest hour was in 1774 when they beat All England by an innings and 52 runs.

The second recorded murder in the village was in 1782 (the first was in 1376). A stranger got into conversation with a local man at the New Inn and during this conversation cut the top off his walking stick. He followed his victim out of the village and then killed him with the stick. He was convicted on the evidence of the piece of stick which he had unwisely left at the inn. The scene of the murder is marked by the Murderstone.

Before the Normandy landings in June 1944 all the lanes and roads right down to the coast were lined with army vehicles. The whole village was sealed off and no one could get out without a pass. May 22nd saw the second recorded royal visitor when King George VI came to review his troops. It was supposed to be a secret but the whole village turned out to watch.

⌘ HANNINGTON

Hannington, a North Hampshire Downs village of outstanding natural beauty

Hannington village green

(with about 280 inhabitants) lies sleepily, sans shops but with one public house, two miles off the A339 between Newbury and Basingstoke. Most people are employed outside the village and since the village school was closed in 1984, the children travel to various schools.

The birthplace of Archbishop Warham, and mentioned in the Domesday Book, Hannington has a beautiful brick and flint-built Norman church of All Saints on the edge of the village green, with wellhead and bench, as well as a small Methodist chapel. Community life today exists through these and other organisations which tend to meet in the village hall.

The community highlight is the Country Fayre and Barbecue when all village members make enormous efforts for this splendid occasion – people travel from Portsmouth to attend!

There are five thatched cottages in Hannington, the one opposite the village green is authenticated as being 14th century and is called Tyn-y-Bryn. The village green, incidentally, was once a pond.

Hannington Silver Band, formed in 1924, does a great deal of charity work and is the pride of the village.

⌘ HARTLEY WINTNEY

Hartley Wintney is a pretty village sitting astride the A30, once a stage coach route. The afternoon coach, the *Telegraph*, ran from the Phoenix Inn to London every day at 1 pm and the *Defiance* left each morning at 8.30. Highwaymen were also known to use the same road holding passengers to ransom for their money and valuables.

Along the road is Hatten's Pond, named for Robert Hatten, landlord of the nearby Waggon and Horses pub from 1875 until his death in 1903. In the centre of this pond is a duck-house with a thatched roof, courtesy of the inhabitants of the village, and at Christmastime it is decorated with fairy lights to match the rest of the illuminations.

Trafalgar oaks stretch across the common, planted long ago to provide wood for shipbuilding, and on the green cricket has been played since 1770. The old field names tell their own story: Sheep Down and Hog Moor were grazing lands beyond tilled soil; Flax-field was where flax, with its lovely pale-blue flowers, was grown, and the stems, soaked and combed, provided the fibres for linen to make the villagers' clothes. Furzy Moor was where teazels were employed to tease the cloth and White Field where the spun and woven cloth was laid to bleach in the sun.

At West Green House once lived Lieutenant-General Henry Hawley, a prominent soldier during the Jacobite Rebellion of 1745. After Culloden when he rivalled Judge Jeffreys for cruelty, he returned to Hartley Wintney, where it's said that on the night of 16th April each year, the anniversary of the battle, the skirl of the pipes and war cries of the Highland clans can be heard in the garden!

The thatched duck-house on the village pond in Hartley Wintney

⌘ HEADLEY

The history of Headley, which lies in the east of the county, dates back to Saxon times and it is mentioned in the Domesday Book, when it was called Hallege.

The church in the village centre has existed since the 12th century, although the first Headley church in Saxon times was completely made of wood. In 1900 Sir Robert Wright gave the church clock in memory of his son, who died at the age of six. On each corner of the clock are the initials of Sir Robert and his wife, their son and the year. In 1935 a peal of six bells was given in memory of Mr and Mrs Charles McAndrew. They gave the village hall to the Women's Institute.

The lychgate was erected to commemorate the Queen's Coronation in 1953. The work was carried out entirely by Headley men under the supervision of Mr Johnson-Burt.

In 1601 Queen Elizabeth I granted a charter for a fair to be held annually on the village green. In 1795 the parishes of Headley, Bramshott and Kingsley combined to build a House of Industry, which is now called the Grange. The terrible conditions in the workhouse led to riots and arson. Some of the culprits were transported to Australia and some were hanged. The Grange later became a private house.

A flourishing chestnut tree is a well-known local landmark in the centre of the village. It was planted by the rector, Rev Laverty. A sovereign coin was buried at its roots.

Headley is an ever-growing and flourishing village. Tennis, cricket, football and bowls are all enjoyed in the recreation grounds. Headley Mill, a famous beauty spot, is still a working mill and its surrounding pond, with the swans and wild fowl, is well worth a visit. Some of the timber in the mill is from the 16th century.

⌘ HIGHCLERE

Highclere lies in the northern part of Hampshire. There is real beauty surrounding the place – a fine view from Chericot of Sidown and Beacon hills and a view from 'Heaven's Gate' on Sidown hill looking down on to Highclere Castle, the home for years of the Herbert family, the Earls of Carnarvon and lords of the manor. The 5th Earl was the great Egyptologist who discovered the tomb of Tutankhamun. Sir Charles Barry, the architect of the Houses of Parliament, and the 3rd Earl of Carnarvon together converted the mansion, which for 800 years had been a home of the Bishops of Winchester, into the present day castle.

There was a prehistoric way across the Downs on the southern boundary and this was a military road. It was once a mere track called Honey Way, and is now the Newbury–Andover road.

During the latter half of the 19th century a wood turner in Highclere made wooden false teeth. No doubt, if the weather was cold, they sounded like castanets!

One of the old Highclere industries was brickmaking. The deep excavations can still be seen where Pyke's brickfields and kilns were situated, from the north-east end of Tubbs Lane to Old Kiln Cottage, The Mount. Mr Pyke lived at Pyke's House, on the corner at the junction of The

Highclere church seen through the trees

Mount and Andover Road. He supplied bricks for the construction of Highclere Castle.

Highclere Street, now a small hamlet, is about one mile from the centre of the present village. It is evident from the centrally placed ancient inn and several medieval and hall-type houses around it, one of which has a 15th century moulded plaster royal coat of arms on it, that this is the original village. The lane to the original church leads from here. The present Highclere has a 19th century church and most of the houses are of the same date. It has virtually no older or ancient buildings.

⌘ HOOK

Neolithic flints, Bronze Age artefacts, Roman pottery, tiles and coins found around Hook show that there has been occupation in the vicinity since Stone Age times. In the late 1700s, Hook was a tiny hamlet with several public houses, a number of ponds and few cottages – the oldest of which is probably the 14th century 'Forge'.

One of these public houses was the White Hart Hotel. It was a staging post at the crossroads of the London to Exeter and Reading to Gosport turnpikes and therefore it attracted a lot of trade to the area. Nearby was a road-wagon station which repaired stagecoaches.

1883 was an important year for Hook because it won its long campaign for a railway station – village life was never quite the same again. The village school, built in 1843 to serve Hook and Newnham, had to be enlarged for the second time in 1896. In 1902 the goods station was added and what had been principally a farming community started to change. Industry arrived in the form of a cornmill, a sawmill and a coal yard. The new railway sidings at Hook also meant that livestock was able to be transported to and from market more easily and Gowers iron foundry was able to move larger items of machinery.

By 1938, Hook needed a new church to serve its growing community and to replace the tin church which had been built in 1886.

The 1960s saw the start of the building of private housing estates. Growth, which had been gradual, increased considerably with the village doubling in size during the 1980s. Hook, which falls in the Hart District, has tried to keep pace with its dramatic increase in population by investing in a new surgery, a larger primary school and a new community hall.

⌘ HORDLE

The original church stood two miles distant from the village, on the cliff, 'in sound of the sea'. In 1830, in response to a petition from the parishioners, the church was dismantled and re-erected on Hordle common. Sad to say, this had again to be rebuilt 40 years later, owing, perhaps, to faulty construction. The third church, an example of mid-Victorian architecture, was consecrated in 1872. Stones from the ancient church can still be found scattered around the parish.

The church of All Saints has always been the hub of village life. This is still evident today. Together with the newly formed Community Association, great efforts are being made to combine the old and the new in the social life of the community.

One or two thatched cottages remain in the village. Building development increased rapidly in the 1960s. Agricultural land was sold and country houses were demolished to make way for housing. The pattern of the village inevitably changed. Early census returns give the population numbers in the region of 400. The latest figure is nearly 5,000.

Past inhabitants of Hordle worked mainly on the land. Some do so today as there are still a few farms and some fine horticultural nurseries.

A well known benefactor of the village was John Collett (1798–1856). Known as the poacher's friend, he was opposed to the Game Laws and frequently paid fines imposed on poachers. A large grey monolith erected to his memory, stands in the churchyard.

Mrs Mary Ann Girling was a strange religious figure who claimed to be immortal. She was foundress of the sect 'The Children of God', nicknamed 'The Shakers' from the manner of showing their religious fervour. Mrs Girling (her followers called her 'Mother') arrived with her disciples at New Forest Lodge, Hordle in 1872, and completely changed the lives of about 170 people, it is claimed, by hypnotism. The group suffered much hardship in the 14 years of existence. Due in large measure to their peculiar beliefs, the Shakers were evicted for failure to pay monies in connection with the property they had occupied. Mrs Girling died in 1886. The few remaining followers kept a dawn vigil at her grave awaiting her resurrection. Three said they saw her spirit rise from the grave.

Smugglers once used Hordle Cliff to watch for danger, for it commands an extensive view of the ocean. The treacherous route along the cliff became a nightmare for a Customs Officer one dark night, when his horse mistook the path and hurtled him down 70 feet toward the sea. Lovey Warne passed this way with her contraband silks and lace bound about her person beneath her crinoline.

⌘ HORNDEAN

Horndean is a village with a population greater than that of its neighbouring town of Petersfield, yet it has no bank and no parish church, though it has a brewery, which celebrated its centenary in 1988, several pubs, an Indian restaurant and a Chinese takeaway.

It has grown enormously since the Second World War and is now bisected by the A3(M). It was not until the 20th century that it became a village of note. In 1903 the Light Railway, which ran from Cosham to Horndean, was opened. The fare was 5d single and 8d return. Trippers would come from Portsmouth for a day's outing in the country. It ceased running at the beginning of 1935 due to unprofitability.

Merchistoun Hall is a Grade II listed building. Not much is known about the Hall before 1800. When Admiral Sir Charles Napier bought it in about 1836 it was called Quallets Grove or, more simply The Grove. He retired there in 1855 and was MP for Southwark until his death in 1860. In his last years he divided his time between experimental farming, becoming an authority on sheep and turnips, and attempting to remedy abuses and discontents in the Navy. He was a well-known figure in the village with his strange dress, ugly gait, strikingly untidy and somewhat repellent appearance and his meddlesome monkey.

In 1978, as a result of a nationwide appeal by the ITV children's programme *Magpie*, Cadlington House was obtained, upgraded and refurbished as a home for severely mentally handicapped children. The New Blendworth Garden Centre has been more recently set up in grounds which were part of the Cadlington estate and is run for the training in horticulture of 32 mentally handicapped young people.

⌘ HURSTBOURNE TARRANT

Hurstbourne Tarrant, which embraces the hamlet of Ibthorpe, originated as a

The timber-framed granary at Hurstbourne Tarrant

Saxon settlement. Most of the higher ground around the village was at one time forested. It was part of the extensive King's Forest and in 1226 this crown property was granted to the Cistercian nunnery of Tarrant in Dorset – hence the present name of Hurstbourne Tarrant.

St Peter's church was built at the end of the 12th century. The font dates from the 13th century and 14th century wall paintings still survive faintly on the north wall. One depicts the 'Morality of the three living and the three dead'; and other 'The Seven Deadly Sins'. In the 14th century the vicar and many of his parishioners died of the plague.

We learn much about conditions in the early 19th century from William Cobbett, who often stayed in the village with Farmer Blount at Rookery Farm while gathering material for his *Rural Rides*. 'In no part of England', he wrote 'have I seen the labouring people so badly off as they are here'. Cheap corn was coming in from the colonies and local farmers could not compete. Two other industries allied to farming helped to sustain the villagers – malting and forestry.

The malthouses not only supplied Andover breweries but became brewhouses in their own right supplying the village inns, of which there were six. The Five Alls stood by the tollgate at the top of Hurstbourne Hill. At the other end of the village was the King's Arms on the Newbury Road. The Coopers' Arms in the centre of the village was destroyed by fire in 1904. Close by was the Plough and, at Ibthorpe, the White Hart, now both private residences. The only remaining inn is the George and Dragon at one time a posting house with stabling.

⌘ ITCHEN ABBAS

Three miles from Alresford, Itchen Abbas lies in the lovely Itchen valley. It is a small rural village with church, primary school, police house and a country pub – the Plough Inn.

The church of St John the Baptist is of Norman design, rebuilt in 1863 on the site of the original church dated 1092. Some of the original stones and part of the chancel arch were used in the rebuilding. In the churchyard a magnificent and stately yew tree, which was possibly a sapling when the first church was built, shades the grave of the gypsy John Hughes, the last man hanged in Winchester in 1825 for horse stealing. He was buried in consecrated ground due to the Christian spirit of the rector, Rev Robert Wright.

There are several old houses in the village. Bignall's Cottage at the top of the hill was the home long ago of Peter Bignall, the village carpenter and wheelwright. He is reputed to have seen the village ghost, a white lady who walked up and down on moonlit nights without her head.

Charles Kingsley often visited Itchen Abbas. He stayed at the old Plough Inn, the predecessor of the present Plough, and immortalised the village in *The Water Babies*. On his visits here he used to fish what he described as 'the loveliest of vale rivers' and in *Hereward the Wake* he described the waters of the Itchen, so clear 'that none could see where water ended and where air began'. Robert Browning also loved Itchen Abbas and wrote his well-known verse *The year's at the spring* as part of his poetic drama *Pippa Passes*.

⌘ ITCHEN STOKE

The village of Itchen Stoke lies east of Itchen Abbas, on the B3047 road to the nearby town of Alresford. There are delightful thatched cottages and later ones built of flint and brick. The old school and schoolhouse built of undressed flint is now a private house and lies at the top of ancient Water Lane, which leads downhill to a once very important ford over the river Itchen. A footpath along the riverbank is much used by people walking to the village of Ovington about a mile away.

On the opposite side of the road is the church of St Mary the Virgin, which lies in the centre of the village. The present church was built in 1866, the design based on that of La Sainte Chapelle in Paris. It is worthy of a visit – there is an ancient font of stone standing on four pillars which was found in pieces in the present churchyard hedge and reassembled by a recent vicar, and the rose windows are beautiful. The pulpit is unusual and can be entered only from the vestry. Although no longer used for regular worship it remains consecrated and is now in the care of the Redundant Churches Fund.

⌘ KINGSCLERE

Watership Down, a name familiar to millions, is part of the downland surrounding Kingsclere, made famous by Richard Adams' novel and now better known than Kingsclere itself. The downs provide an undulating green backdrop to the village. An excellent spot for flying kites and model aeroplanes, a venue for archery and horse riding events and the Wayfarer's Walk attracts ramblers. Tourists who seek the background to the story are likely to be confronted by racehorses on training gallops, flocks of sheep, exhaltations of skylarks, but rabbits are fairly rare.

A village that is steeped in history, named Kings Clere at the beginning of the 13th century, it has received royal patronage since Saxon times. The 12th century parish church has a unique weather-vane, traditionally identified as a bed bug, ordered to be exhibited by King John after a bad night at the local inn!

The fast pace of modern life has changed the face of Kingsclere. A bypass has channelled the traffic away from the centre of the village, and oak-beamed 16th century houses, no long fretted by dust and fumes, have been renovated and colourwashed and are interspersed with new houses and courtyards built in traditional style.

In the 19th century there were ten public houses, a number now reduced to three. During restoration work at the Swan, a 15th century roof was discovered, with beams coated with soot from centuries of fires that burned in the centre of the floor.

A golf course and a small industrial estate are recent additions to the village and provide some local employment. The village was once almost self-sufficient, with a diversity of employment in agriculture, brewing, rope-making, tanning, milling and building.

The clear chalk stream that runs through the village supports a variety of wildlife. A new footpath makes it possible to enjoy the quiet beauty of the stream in the very centre of the village. Seats and flowerbeds have been set out in the village square and the magnificent Victorian lamp standard removed in 1969 in favour of a modern one, has been restored and returned to grace the square once more.

⌘ KINGS SOMBORNE

The Sombornes lie in the low hills on the edge of the beautiful Test valley. Up Somborne is a ribbon of houses some three miles from the main village, and Little Somborne is scattered around an enchanting small chapel of Saxon origin.

Kings Somborne

Kings Somborne, known to walkers as it lies on the intersection of the Test and Clarendon Ways, has probably never been so pretty, as affluence and paint have brightened its buildings. Barely 40 years ago the impression was tumbledown and shabby. The shortsighted policy then was to destroy unfit buildings rather than repair them, so some character has gone from the village. There is still one pub and a few shops, and the ecclesiastical parish is unusual in that it is joined only with nearby Ashley. The church of St Peter and St Paul, basically Norman, was regrettably rebuilt in 1885. It and the pub stand pleasantly on a mini-green, complete with war memorial.

The 'Kings' of the village name were Saxon. Somborne was a royal manor before the Norman Conquest, then, in medieval times, it was the centre of its Hundred and Deanery. It remained a royal possession until sold by Charles II. The boundary of John of Gaunt's deer park is still marked in places by a bank and yew trees.

The village achieved fame in the midst of the agricultural depression that beset rural Hampshire in the mid 19th century. In 1837 Richard Dawes, blocked by his liberal views from an academic career, was appointed to the living of Kings Somborne. He found a parish run down and demoralised, so in the belief that education would improve social and moral conditions he organised a school, which opened in October 1842. He believed that the school should be self-supporting and that teaching should be practical and interesting and of evident benefit to everyone – views much ahead of his time. By 1847, the school was one of the best-known in the country, and it was visited by the Prime Minister, Mathew Arnold and Florence Nightingale. Dawes became Dean of Hereford in 1850. The school continues in the same building today.

⌘ LASHAM

The tiny village of Lasham adjoins Herriard, and for about 200 years was part of the Herriard Park estate. We know from the records of Herriard and other villages how the name has changed over the centuries. In Lasham it is happening in our lifetime, not so much in the spelling, but in the pronunciation. Until about 20 years ago it was called "Lassum', but more and more it is called 'Lash-am'. No doubt in another 20 years 'Lassum' will have passed into the history books.

During the First World War, Mrs Beatrice Jervoise managed Church Farm at Lasham. She was so concerned by the shortage of water that she brought in a dowser. His findings were so successful that Major and Mrs Jervoise were able to found the Herriard and Lasham Water Company, with reservoirs in Lasham Wood. This enabled water to be piped to Lasham, Herriard, Shalden, Bentworth, Wield, Tunworth, Weston Corbett, Ellisfield, Medstead, Bradley and Preston Candover. This remarkable feat is recorded on Mrs Jervoise' tomb in Herriard churchyard.

The village pond in Lasham is fed from local springs

Although such a small village, Lasham is known throughout the country for its gliding club, the National Gliding Championships often being held at Lasham Airfield. The airfield was built during the Second World War, when the beautiful beech avenue planted by George Jervoise in 1809 was sacrificed to make way for it. The old road between Herriard and Lasham was closed, and gangs of Irish labourers and Italian prisoners of war were brought in to make the 'concrete road' which is now part of the A339.

The village is justly proud of its pretty pond, which is fed from local springs. It is regularly cleaned out, and is the home of mallard and moorhens, as well as large numbers of goldfish.

⌘ LAVERSTOKE & FREEFOLK

The parish of Laverstoke and Freefolk was united in 1872, when, on the closure of St Mary's in Laverstoke Park, the tiny 13th century church of St Nicholas became the parish church. St Mary's in the Park then became the vaults of the Portal family. In 1896 a new church named St Mary the Virgin was built, dominating the village of Freefolk.

Portal's Mills originated in 1712, when Henri de Portal, a French refugee, landed with others at Southampton. He was eventually offered an apprenticeship at Stoneham, and on completion he became naturalised. He then acquired the lease of Bere Mill, where he perfected papermaking. As he progressed he needed to expand, so he applied for Laverstoke Mill, and built a new mill on the site in 1718. In 1724 the Bank of England requested him to submit samples for use as banknote paper. It was approved and the contract still exists, amid strict security. The production takes place at Overton Mill, two miles to the east, which one of Henri's successors, Sir William Portal, built in 1922. A great deal of its success is derived from the river Test, which rises at Ashe a mile upstream. After use and recycling the water then flows on through Laverstoke, Freefolk and on to Southampton Water.

Lord Portal, who died in 1949, was Head of the Olympic Games when it was held in Germany in 1936, and as a mark of respect for his services to the Games, Hitler awarded him the Iron Cross. In 1948 the Olympic Committee honoured Lord Portal by allowing the Olympic Flame to be carried by a runner through the Park.

Lord Portal had 18 thatched cottages built in memory of his father Sir William Portal, for the use of employees in Freefolk. A white house in Laverstoke bears a plaque indicating that it was the residence of the Bank Officer, 1785, built by Jospeh Portal.

⌘ LIPHOOK

Six roads converge on the Square in the centre of Liphook and in the early days of the 20th century there were hardly any houses along them. Now there are blocks of flats tucked into every conceivable corner.

On the northern boundary the river Wey winds through water meadows, which in olden days were flooded regularly in order to provide a second cereal crop. This area has now been restored to parkland, which serves as a much needed recreational facility for the residents of the village.

The village carnival, which takes place in October each year, started life as an 'Old Boys' Bonfire Club', which celebrated the anniversary of the Gunpowder Plot. In the beginning it was simply a bonfire made from wood cut and collected by 'the boys' of the community, but it evolved into pranks being played upon other residents and gradually the Carnival came into being. When a chimney sweep by the name of Stacy entered a float depicting a model of his cottage, which sported an advertisement and had a brush sticking out of the chimney, the character of the procession changed. Today the event attracts floats from all sections of the community.

The square, which is dominated by the Royal Anchor Hotel, is a designated conservation area and some of the old houses and shops are still there, even if the smithy is not. People who need to have their horses shod rely on travelling blacksmiths, who set up their equipment wherever it is required, usually in the open fields.

Liphook boasts of having Flora Thompson, the authoress of *Lark Rise to Candleford*, as one of its celebrities. She used to be the local post-mistress. The post office was once housed in a building completely on its own. It is now only a counter in a local supermarket. What would Flora have said?

⌘ LONGPARISH

Towards the end of the 10th century the area known as Longparish was in fact the manor of Middleton (or Middletune). The manor was in the possession of the Benedictine nunnery of Wherwell, which was founded in AD 986 by Elfrida, widow of King Edgar, who was indirectly responsible for the murder of her step-son King Edward at Corfe. Lower Mill House was originally a cloth mill known as 'Middletune Mill' and belonged to the abbess of Wherwell. Middletune Mill is mentioned in the Domesday Book.

The name Longparish first appears in the middle of the 16th century, at about the time of the Dissolution of the Monasteries, when it was said to consist of East Aston, Longparish, Middleton and Forton and the greater part of Harewood Forest.

In Harewood Forest there is a monument known as Deadman's Plack. In the year AD 963, King Edgar, called the Peaceable, sent for the Earl Athelwold to meet him in the forest to hunt. Athelwold had betrayed Edgar and had married his intended bride, Elfrida, daughter of the Earl of Devonshire. So Edgar slew Athelwold with his own hand.

Cricket at Longparish has a long and checkered history, stretching from the first memorable match in 1878. In 1980 Longparish reached the final of the Whitbread Village Cricket Championship, and on 24th August they went to play their opponents Marchwiel from North Wales on the hallowed ground of Lords, but sadly they lost. However, on Monday 31st August 1987 Longparish played in the final again, against Treeton Welfare from Yorkshire. Longparish won by 76 runs and returned home with the cup to the celebrations of the village.

⌘ LONGSTOCK

Longstock is well named. Stoke or stock means a place with stakes or wooden piles, often a place with a timber bridge – and the village is about three miles long. It was recorded in the 1086 Domesday Book as Stoches.

The list of known vicars begins in 1315, although there was a church here before that. The present church of St Mary, however, dates from 1880. Nowadays the rector of Stockbridge is also vicar of Longstock and of Leckford.

The river Test at Longstock

In the 19th century most of the inhabitants worked on the many local farms: Upper Manor, Lower Manor, Charity, Church, Waters Down, Westover, Windover and Hazeldown. Over 40 day-labourers would wait at the sharp bend near Corner Cottage and hope to get a day's employment. In 1865 the village had two blacksmiths, two builders, two beer retailers, two landlords, a horse-trainer, a baker and a grocer, a shoemaker, a maltster, a wheelwright, a postmaster, a miller, a brick-layer, a shopkeeper and a schoolmistress. There was also an unusual cottage industry – the making of baskets and mats from the sedge grass growing on the banks of the river Test. Children were set to plait the prepared sedge and the women formed the plaits into rush mats and light baskets.

From the middle to the end of the 19th century, Stockbridge race-course, which lay in Longstock parish under Danebury Hill, was, with Ascot and Goodwood, a very fashionable affair. The then Prince of Wales, later King Edward VII, regularly rented Hermit Lodge, a Regency house just down Houghton Road, at Longstock's southern end. Miss Lillie Langtry, a well-known actress of the period, also rented a house in Stockbridge for the race weeks. The gardens lie on opposite banks of the Test and are still joined by a private footbridge. The race course was closed when it was inherited by a lady who did not approve of gambling.

⌘ LYNDHURST

The village of Lyndhurst is known as the capital of the New Forest. Written as Linhest in 1086, its name is derived from the linden or lime tree, 'hurst' being a wooded hillock. Perhaps of Jutish origin, the village was ancient when Canute demonstrated at nearby Southampton that even a king could not rule the waves. A few years later another king, William of Normandy (the Conqueror) visited Lyndhurst while enjoying his hunting.

Of the few really old buildings still extant in Lyndhurst, the best known is the Queen's House. This handsome brick building is now occupied by the Forestry Commission. Attached to the Queen's House is the Verderers' Court

Lyndhurst

with a history going back hundreds of years. The present court, as now constituted, dates from 1949, but it still has the power to deny Lyndhurst its urgently needed bypass. The heavy commercial and commuter traffic passing through the High Street is the only blight to the village.

The offices of the New Forest District Council are situated in Lyndhurst. At Foxlease the Girl Guides Association Centre entertains Guides from all over the world. The Hampshire Police Force are represented by a large modern police station.

Churches supply the need of three denominations. The largest, St Michael's, an imposing brick building, contains a famous fresco by Lord Leighton and windows by Burne-Jones and William Morris. In the churchyard is the grave of Alice Hargreaves, for whom, when a little girl, *Alice in Wonderland* was written.

There is a golf course and a very old cricket ground. The beautiful little mound known as 'Boltons Bench' hill, makes a perfect grandstand for cricket spectators and attracts skiers and tobogganists in winter. The opposite end of the village to Boltons Bench is Swan Green, world famous for its picturesque thatched cottages, often depicted on picture postcards.

⌘ MARTIN & DAMERHAM

Martin and Damerham are tucked away in the 'Martin Peninsula' in the far west of the county, surrounded on three sides by Wiltshire and Dorset. It is an area of

The old village pump still stands on the green in Martin

outstanding beauty and steeped in history, with many burial mounds, Roman remains and roads, ancient earthworks and the famous Bockerley Ditch, built about 1,600 years ago.

Martin (Mertone in the 10th century) is a linear village with grass banks and some fine thatched cottages. It is the 'Winterbourne Bishop' of W. H. Hudson's book *A Shepherd's Life*, the story of a Victorian countryman.

All Saints' church, set behind the village, dates back to the 12th century. There is also a Methodist Chapel but no public house. There is a club though, a post office and a village hall.

Damerham is set on the Allen river, more a stream, which rises above Martin. After many meanderings and change of name, it flows into the Avon at Fordingbridge.

St George's church, on a hill on the edge of the village, was built around the time of the Norman Conquest. This is just one of four churches which are in the Western Downland benefice, the other three being Martin, Rockbourne and Whitsbury.

The thriving village school is one half of the only Federated School in Hampshire. The other half is in the village of Rockbourne two miles away. Children from both sites meeting together regularly.

The village pub, the Compasses, is a popular meeting place for villagers and visitors to the area. They used to brew their own beer as well.

⌘ MEONSTOKE, EXTON & CORHAMPTON

When the Danes invaded southern England they came up the now much smaller river Meon in their longboats, and a battle against the local farming Saxons took place in Meonstoke. Some Danes subsequently settled in Meonstoke and there was friction for hundreds of years with the farmers across the river in Exton and Corhampton.

Corhampton church was built in about 1020 and is one of the very few small Saxon churches which has always functioned as an active church. Its dedication is unknown but part of the frescoes remaining in the chancel depict St Swithun restoring the dropped eggs to the widow's basket. In the churchyard, a 1,000 year old yew tree still stands, protecting some unusual vaulted brick graves and shadowing the old sundial on the church wall, which is divided into eight tides, not twelve hours.

As the people 'across the water' did not speak to each other, each village had its

Old Winchester Hill, a favourite spot for walkers

own footpath to Bishop's Waltham. The bridge into Exton was not built until 1805. Where the present pub, the Shoe, now stands was the wheelwright's workshop. The old Shoe was a tiny pub in the garden opposite next to the river, which sometimes flooded in spite of the sluice and mill 50 yards upstream. Corhampton and Meonstoke also had their mills, as each village had to be quite self-contained.

The north outlet from Exton onto the A32 is known as The Grinch, but whether the word has any bearing on the fact that a gibbet was sited there is not known. Very close by a Roman villa was recently excavated; and in the same field Saxon bones were found. In one lucky dig a complete warrior lying straight was found with his sword by his side and his circular shield boss on his chest.

The South Downs Way long distance footpath comes through Exton and the Wayfarers Walk comes through Droxford and the back of Corhampton and Exton on its way from Emsworth to Inkpen Beacon. There are several other footpaths and pleasant walks around the villages up to Beacon Hill to the west and Old Winchester Hill, an Iron Age fort, to the east, both commanding extensive views.

⌘ MICHELDEVER

Motorists from Popham, driving along the A30, feel that they have some

Dulce Street, Micheldever

knowledge of Micheldever, a mere scattering of buildings, whilst those on the A33 from the same point are under the same impression. Travellers by train stopping at Micheldever station are even more deceived, especially as they are aware of the oil terminal and can see a pleasant early Victorian building on one of the platforms, while an elegant Georgian building stands outside the station yard. It is therefore a revelation to some who venture a few miles off these routes to discover the lovely and interesting village of Micheldever itself. Over half the dwellings are over a hundred years old, many of them thatched, while the newer ones, with well-kept gardens, fit snugly into the overall pattern of well-loved homes.

The village, together with East Stratton, has been fortunate with its benefactors. Lady Rachel Vaughan who lived at East Stratton House, presented the church of St Mary the Virgin with a silver chalice. Later benefactors have been the Barings, and more recently, Lord Rank, who farmed in this area and resided at Sutton Scotney.

There are several farms in the vicinity, so some people work on the land and with animals, some at the watercress beds and others commute to Winchester, Basingstoke and London. In late summer, the village is alive with tractors pulling loaded wagons of grain to and from the dryer.

Refreshment is obtainable in Micheldever at the Half Moon and Spread Eagle, a fine Georgian building standing on a piece of rising ground on Gin Hill. East Stratton boasts the Plough, attractively rural and used gratefully by walkers among others. The Dove at the station is popular for its cuisine and is quite well known outside the village.

⌘ NEW ALRESFORD

New Alresford is an attractive market town in the heart of Hampshire, which draws thousands of visitors each year. There are three main streets, Broad Street, East Street and West Street and they are laid out very much as they were when plans were made by Bishop Godfrey de Lucy in about 1200. It takes its name from the river Arle which flows between Old and New Alresford. Near the parish boundary the Arle is joined by the Candover and Tichborne streams, the three forming the river Itchen which flows on to Winchester.

Broad Street is justly famous as one of the most beautiful streets in Hampshire, and is planted with lime trees and with lighting from old-style lamps which have been refurbished. Mary Russell Mitford, the authoress of *Our Village*, lived in Broad Street when she was a child and another house bears a plaque proclaiming that the 47th Infantry Regiment of the United States Army made their headquarters there during the Second World War in the run up to D-Day.

The Watercress Steam Railway draws thousands of visitors each year, eager to travel on the line from Alresford through Ropley and Medstead to Alton. A favourite walk is along the river which goes past the charming old Fulling Mill.

Attractive houses along Broad Street in New Alresford

Another popular walk is out past Town Mill and the watercress beds to Old Alresford, walking along the Little Weir and returning along the Great Weir alongside Alresford Pond.

There are many old tombstones in the churchyard of St John's, but four in particular are worthy of note. They are the graves of French prisoners of war. From 1808 to 1814, during the Napoleonic Wars, there were something like 200 prisoners on parole in Alresford. Some died here and were buried in the churchyard, and their gravestones are still cared for.

⌘ NORTH BADDESLEY

The original name of 'Bedeslei' is thought to be a derivation of Baeddes Leah, 'Baeddi's Wood' or clearing. There are signs of Roman and Saxon settlements within the area. In medieval times, the centre of the village was the parish church of St John the Baptist (still its most cherished possession), and the manor house, which was a Preceptory for the Knights Hospitallers of St John of Jerusalem from around 1167.

There are two gravestones in the churchyard both bearing the same name. In 1822 Robert Snelgrove, an assistant keeper on the Broadlands estate belonging to Lord Palmerston, found two men poaching at Toot-hill. One of the men, Charles Smith, fired when the keeper was close at hand and wounded him seriously in the thigh. Both men got away but many months later Smith was caught and condemned to death at Winchester Assizes. Palmerston did his utmost to get the sentence reduced to one of imprisonment but failed and Smith was duly hanged. The first gravestone was erected by William Cobbett, writer and social reformer of the time, who felt that Smith had been a victim of oppression. The second gravestone appeared many years after Lord Palmerston's death

Charles Smith's two gravestones at North Baddesley

and was erected by his grandson, Evelyn Ashley, in an attempt to absolve the family from any blame.

Street names in the village have generally been adopted from the families who owned the manor of Baddesley: Seymour Parade after the famous Tudor family; Mortimer Drive commemorates the Earls of March who held the manor in the reign of Richard II; Chamberlayne Court after the last recent owners; and Tottehale Close and Launcelyn Close are taken from the Preceptors of the Knights Hospitallers.

⌘ OLD ALRESFORD

The village of Old Alresford, on the ancient route from Winchester to London, is just north of Alresford. A great fire in 1160 destroyed the original village. This was rebuilt by Bishop De Lucy who also made the causeway connecting it with his new town of New Market, now known as New Alresford. This causeway, commonly known as the Great Weir, is the greatest medieval construction in England still serving its original purpose as both road and a dam.

Nearby at Abbotstone are the visible remains of a deserted village. The community was affected by the Black Death in 1349 to 1350, but it started to finally decline in the 18th century when large numbers of agricultural workers deserted the countryside for the towns.

Old Alresford Place, now a Diocesan Retreat Centre, was occupied at the time of the Civil War by the rector, Dr Heylyn, a fervent Royalist. He was driven from his rectory by his neighbour, the Cromwellian Colonel Norton. Oliver Cromwell often stayed with Colonel Norton, whose local knowledge was an important factor in the victory over the Royalists, fighting over unknown territory, in the decisive battle of Cheriton.

In St Mary's church is a memorial to Mary Sumner, who founded the Mothers Union in 1875, now a world-wide organisation. The original meetings were held in the drawing room of the then rectory, now Old Alresford Place.

The watercress industry plays a major part in the local economy due to the clear running Hampshire chalk streams and the constant water temperature. The attractive village green is now registered as common land. A generous resident bought the land for the village and with other volunteer residents built drainage chambers from which the spring water is piped into the brook.

The Cricket Club is over 100 years old and for many years has played on the lovely ground on Bighton Lane by courtesy of the owner of Upton Park.

⌘ OVERTON

Overton lies either side of the famous trout river, the Test, on the B3400 between

The White Hart Inn in the centre of Overton

Basingstoke and Andover. It was a 'church' manor from at least the time of King Alfred and is mentioned in the Domesday Book. The original settlement was on the north bank of the river and the church building dates back to the late Norman period. The White Hart Inn at the main crossroads in the village was a coaching inn on the old stage coach route from London to Exeter. In the 19th century, sheep fairs were held annually in the wide thoroughfare called Winchester Street and this is still the site today for Overton's summer carnival activities.

Since 1920 Overton has been the home of Portals Limited – a company which produces banknotes and security paper for world markets. People who live in Overton work here or in nearby towns, and increasing numbers commute to London. The population has increased and new housing areas have arisen. Shops in the High Street and Winchester Street are numerous and varied, and there are restaurants, pubs and clubs for evening entertainment.

Overton has its own primary school and playschool but it is the abundance and variety of leisure organisations which thrive here that promotes the friendly and caring atmosphere of the village and welcomes newcomers. There are Cubs, Scouts and Guides, clubs for local history, dramatics, photography, senior citizens, the Women's Institute and evening classes at the school, to mention just a few. The recreation centre – built on an area of drained marsh in front of the church – caters for almost every sport from Rugby and golf to netball and archery.

⌘ PAMBER HEATH

The village of Pamber Heath is situated in north Hampshire close to the Berkshire border. It is six miles from Basingstoke and, with Pamber End and Pamber Green, is part of the parish of Pamber. St Luke's church forms the centre of the village along with a large village hall, opened in the late 1970s and paid for by fund raising from the local people.

The name Pamber, originally spelled Pambeare, goes back to Norman times, the addition of 'Heath' coming in later centuries.

Henry de Port founded Pamber Priory in the 12th century, and its remains stand today as a reminder of the time when this was one of the most important monastic establishments in Hampshire.

The three Pambers are surrounded by open lands: Silchester common, Tadley common and the extensive Pamber Forest, an ancient woodland. Pamber Forest is a nature reserve of some 478 acres and designated a Site of Special Scientific Interest. Hazel, chestnut and oak have been coppiced for many years, and the structure of the woodland varies from dry open heathland through to dense hazel, to streams lined with alders and willows. The forest is home to many species of butterfly, some 30 species have been recorded. Bat boxes can be seen high up on some trees, to provide a home for the bats that choose to live in the forest. Flora, insects, small mammals and birds all make the forest their home, as do roe deer and fallow deer. Snakes, especially adders, are in abundance and can often be seen basking in the warm sunshine.

⌘ PENNINGTON

Pennington is situated on the south coast of Hampshire, one mile west of the historic town of Lymington. The parish of St Mark, Pennington is divided into three parts – Upper, Centre and Lower Pennington.

In Upper Pennington is to be found the common which gave the village the nickname of 'Donkey Town', as large numbers of donkeys used to graze there. Nowadays a few goats are to be seen, but the common's use now is recreational, and each year the village is visited by a circus and a fair.

The salterns have existed on the marshes at Lower Pennington from early times. At one time there were 13 saltworks, but now only paddling pools for children remain. The marshes are a haven for birdlife, birdwatchers and walkers. It is possible to walk from Pennington to Lymington or Keyhaven along the sea wall. Commander Peter Ouvry, who lived at the 'Salterns', was the first person to dismantle a magnetic mine in the Second World War, which enabled the Allies to find a defence against it.

Pennington marshes

In the centre of the village is Jubilee Cottage in Wainsford Road. Built in 1897 by the lord of the manor to commemorate Queen Victoria's Diamond Jubilee, it was originally the soup kitchen, but was converted to a dwelling in the 1930s. Yarrell Cottage in Ramley Road, which overlooks the common is a very old building, and was at one time an inn called the Cricketers Arms. King's Huts at Upper Pennington were built by Mrs Powell King of Wainsford in 1908. These six cottages are in the shape of a horseshoe. The unusual interior design was Mrs Powell King's own idea, on the advice of Sir Edward Lutyens. Yaldhurst Lodge, which is found at the end of a private road off Ramley Road, was mentioned in the Domesday Book.

⌘ QUARLEY

Quarley lies north of Grateley, and is a neighbouring parish. Whereas Grateley derives its name from the 'great lea', Quarley derives its name from a quarter of the lea. It has a manor house and a church which are mentioned in the Domesday Book. A feature of St Michael's is that three church bells are housed in a frame, with a roof over it, in the churchyard.

The village hall was built and opened in 1987, due mainly to fund raising efforts

The church bells stand outside the church in Quarley

by the villagers. The school, which was built in 1817 for 36 pupils, is now a private house and the children of the village go to Amport school.

The village used to have a public house, but this was destroyed by fire in the late 1920s. The Marquis of Winchester, who then owned virtually the whole village, gave the villagers a choice of a new pub or a water supply for the village. The villagers chose the water supply, and an artesian well was dug, with a water tower. Hence the villagers who wanted something stronger walked across the fields to the Plough Inn at Grateley.

Quarley is still a small village, although a few new houses have been built over the last few years, but it remains fairly quiet and unspoiled, with a great community spirit.

⌘ ROMSEY

Many people associate Romsey with Lord and Lady Mountbatten and the Broadlands Estate, but there is much else besides in this close-knit rural community.

The Town Hall has an air of belonging about it with an imposing wrought iron lamp bracket. Past the Town Hall towards the Abbey United Reformed Church you may pause a moment to admire the arch, a relic of a more leisurely period. If you take the road to your left, Abbey Water will lead you to a small garden on the left which is not larger than 15 feet square, but where one can sit a while and admire the houses along Abbey Water.

After your rest, take a good look at the first house; it was obviously on the corner of two thoroughfares as its angled front suggests. Follow the angle upward and read the sign which is still visible on the side of the house, proclaiming:

> THOS. ELY and SONS
> Whitesmiths   Gasfitters
> Tinsmiths and Glaziers

Proceed along Abbey Water with its picturesque houses on your left; opposite, beyond the railing, is a pond with shrubs and vines rampant on the bank. This quiet backwater leads to Narrow Lane which wanders away to the left. Turn right and proceed through another arch for five yards before turning left once again. Continue along this road; if you wish to visit the Abbey turn right, otherwise continue straight along the road to the bridge which spans the river Test.

In front of you is Rivermead House. Note the chair cut from the stump of a tree which had stood on the pavement in front of the house. The seat is quite comfortable and allows a few moments contemplation before entering the Memorial Gardens, a tranquil spot with a view of carefully tended colourfully planted areas.

Retrace your steps to the Abbey and continue along the paved walk, admiring

Romsey's colourful Square

the magnificent doors as you pass, and go on towards the market place. Turn left and proceed along the north side until you reach The White Horse, an old coaching inn which retains much of its original structure when viewed from the market place.

When next you visit Romsey, and can spare time to wander down the out-of-the-way side roads and lanes, you may be pleasantly surprised and delighted.

⌘ ST MARY BOURNE

St Mary Bourne is in the Hampshire Highlands, the highest points of the southern range of the South Downs running a little distance away to the north of the parallel Bourne valley. The Bourne, from which three villages on its bank take their name, is an intermittent chalk stream. The volume of water has undoubtedly lessened over the centuries. Some are inclined to attribute this to springs tapped for the nearby watercress beds.

The original church of St Peter was probably a Norman building without aisles. Of this, the only parts now remaining are the chancel arch and the responds of the tower, which are of the late Norman period. The church contains several items of considerable historic interest, including what is undoubtedly one of Hampshire's greatest antique treasures – a massive font, carved eight centuries ago from black

73

St Mary Bourne

Tournai marble. An ancient part of the church has a recumbent effigy in stone of an armoured knight, whose crossed legs indicate that he had been a Crusader.

In the centre of the village is the Summerhaugh, used for festivities such as May Day, when it was decorated with hawthorn in flower, and dances took place round a maypole. The name Summerhaugh probably comes from a place by the stream where the cattle were brought down from the hill slopes in summer into an enclosure surrounded by a hedge, 'haga'.

One of the oldest houses in the Bourne valley is Butlers, a mellow brick and beam building in Gangbridge Lane. In alterations made there recently a beam dated 1590 was discovered. Another thatched cottage of interest is Mundays, which used to be the home of a rope maker. There are certainly other houses in the village dating from the early 17th century.

⌘ SELBORNE

This small Hampshire village is known internationally as the birthplace of Gilbert White, the great and famous naturalist. His book, *The Natural History and Antiquities of Selborne*, is recognised as a classic of natural science and English writing.

Gilbert White was born here, in his grandfather's vicarage in 1720. He was ordained as a priest after graduating from Oriel College, Oxford, but was never inducted as vicar of Selborne as the living then was held by Magdalen College. During his lifetime in Selborne, as well as studying and writing about the natural world, he took a great interest in the village school which had been started by his grandfather.

Although there have been many changes in the village over the years, much of Gilbert White's Selborne is still recognisable today – Selborne Hanger, the Common, the Plestor (the old name for the village green), the hollow lanes and the two streams. For the enjoyment of future generations much of Gilbert White's countryside is now owned and cared for by the National Trust.

The main road through the village is very busy and like many other villages,

Selborne seen from the famous Hanger

Selborne has suffered greatly with the noise of heavy lorries passing through. Such was the concern that it was necessary to have a 'lorry watch', to check on all lorries passing through the village. Eventually the Department of Environment banned lorries over 7.5 tonnes from using this road.

Selborne has two thriving pubs, three equally thriving shops, including a post office, a good village hall, sports pavilion and ground, all managed and maintained by voluntary committees. The village hall has recently been renovated, thousands of pounds being raised by various fund-raising activities for this purpose. The sports pavilion too was built by funds raised by an enthusiastic body of local inhabitants.

⌘ SHERBORNE ST JOHN

The name Sherborne probably means 'clear stream' and certainly there is a stream running through, and no less than three duckponds. There has been a settlement here for a very long time and Roman remains have been found in many places.

The Vyne in Sherborne St John boasts a fine classical portico (taken by kind permission of the National Trust)

It must have been larger too, as at one time there were seven alehouses. Now there is only one, the Swan, which is over 500 years old and is still thatched. Just round the corner from the Swan stands the Haye. This has one of Lutyens' earliest extensions and it is said that you can tell it is Lutyens' work because you can't see out of the windows! It was once a Quaker meeting house and some of their graves have been found not only in the garden and under the kitchen floor but in the grounds of the school next door.

At Numbers 6 and 8 West End is a rare example of a Wealdon house, of the kind which is usually found in Kent and Sussex. It is thought to be unique in Hampshire and dates back to 1450. Next door to this is Cleeves, which used to be the village brewhouse but which is now a pleasant home. Legend has it that hidden in a well in the garden is the treasure of Vasco da Gama, though what he could have been doing here is difficult to imagine!

The beautiful village church of St Andrew dates back in part to 1150. After the siege of Basing House, Cromwell is supposed to have given two of Basing's bells to Sherborne St John. Whether this is true or not is unknown, but it is a fact that Sherborne has two pre-Reformation bells and Basing has none. There is also a chained *Foxe's Book of Martyrs* which is rare in a village church. A most entertaining stone stands by the church porch and is to the memory of George Hickson who:–

> '.... had lived above 20 years in the service of William Chute Esq. as whipper in and huntsman and continued after he died in the family as coachman....'

He may not really have been a phantom coachman but there is a ghostly coach and horses which was last seen on the Kingsclere road in 1944. This is Smith Grindle who returns from time to time to search for his treasure in Smith's Green, not to mention the exorcism which was performed in 1923 to stop the rattling of chains in Church Path.

⌘ SOUTH HAYLING

The oldest building in South Hayling is the parish church of St Mary the Virgin. Building began in 1225 and the fabric remains today almost as the original builders left it.

One of Hayling's profitable trades in the olden days was smuggling. They used to start out on a dark night from the ferry in a four-oared gig and row over to France, and it is said they had specially made canvas bags for brandy which would be hung from ladies' crinolines and so transported to their destination.

The number of 'real tennis' courts in the British Isles is small. The one on Hayling opened in 1912, built by Mr R. F. Marshall. There is also a tennis war memorial, now in the gallery of the club house.

A large East Coast oyster company constructed oyster beds at Salterns Creek at the end of the 19th century. The oysters were dredged up from the large beds in the Solent, brought into the creek and preserved there for the winter. A terrible winter in 1901 froze them all and the local industry died out soon after.

After the First World War Commander David Joel and his wife started a business building wooden houses. They were the pioneers of Empire Wood near

Sunrise over Hayling

Hayling station. After many appearances at the Ideal Home exhibitions they left Hayling to open a factory near London.

The golf club was founded in 1883. The Royal Hotel served as the club house until the club was able to build its own. The Hayling Island golf club can boast of having the first lady captain in England. This was Mrs Howard Fairhough, who captained the ladies' golf team in about 1885. She was also the first woman to win a ladies' golf competition in England.

⌘ SOUTHWICK

Southwick is a very small, very old village. In 1988 the owner of the village and estate of Southwick, Mrs Eva Borthwick-Norton, died in her nineties and left it complete to a nephew, Mr R. Thistlethwaite.

The first mention of Southwick was in 1150 when the Augustinian friars found that the priory they had built at Portchester in 1129 was too small. Southwick priory itself was never very large but it was extremely influential at times, indeed the church which now is incorporated in Portsmouth Cathedral was in the

The village green, Southwick

priory's possession. The village church is known as 'St James without the Priory Gates', which indicates it belonged to Southwick rather than the priory.

At the Dissolution of the Monasteries, the priory and its possessions were given to a John White and the estate has passed down more or less intact since then. By the beginning of the 20th century everything in the village – school, churches, shops, pubs, as well as all the houses, belonged to 'The Squire' and so it has remained. Only the 'Big House' and the Park have gone – to the government.

A major event of the 20th century was the planning of Operation Overlord, D-Day, in 1944 at Southwick House. Southwick House was acquired by the Ministry of Defence and remains as HMS Dryad. HMS Dryad is very much part of Southwick and the Navy and the village work amicably together.

The village is most attractive. Because of its single ownership all the woodwork of the cottages and smaller houses is painted the same colour. A stroll down West Street (one of the two streets) takes in five centuries of architecture – from a wattle and daub thatched cottage to Victorian flint houses. Most noticeable are the houses by the green – Tudor cottages mainly, and the 'Terrace', which runs from the Old Post Office to the Red Lion. The two pubs are both 'Lions', the Red and the Golden.

⌘ SPARSHOLT & LAINSTON

Through the centuries the histories of Sparsholt and Lainston have always been interwoven but there is one past inhabitant and benefactor who had quite a considerable bearing on the day to day lives of the villagers.

It was a Mr Samuel Bostock, a barrister formerly of Lainston House, who finally managed to organise a reliable water supply for the area. Before this, the villagers obtained their water from a variety of wells in and around the parishes of Sparsholt and Lainston. The chief supply came from the village well, which relied upon one or two people walking a treadmill for an arduous 20 minutes or so, to draw water from 247 feet below ground. As if this were not problem enough, long hot summers could cause the well to dry up, and villagers were known to cart barrels into Winchester in order to draw water from the river Itchen.

In 1897, to mark Queen Victoria's Jubilee, a new well house was built which disposed of the old well house and the treadmill within. In its place a brick building was erected to house a wind-assisted pump. However, over the years this still did not prove very satisfactory. Fires were frequent and several thatched cottages burned down because the water pressure was not strong enough for fire fighting. So in 1908, Mr Bostock arranged for a piped supply from Crabwood Reservoir to service Sparsholt and Lainston, as well as the neighbouring village of Littleton. The well house can still be seen today opposite the church.

The site of the village hall is again due to the generous benevolence of Samuel Bostock, and the land for the village cricket ground was donated in the same way,

The ruined church viewed from Lainston House

with the only interruption for its use coming during the war years when it was converted to a bowling green. This was presumably due to the fact that most of the men from the village were away fighting for King and Country. Today, Sparsholt Cricket Club still plays on the same ground in Locks Lane.

⌘ STOCKBRIDGE

Stockbridge is an interesting village to linger in. Its long street of small shops includes cosy little teashops, and a hotel with a room which projects out into the street over an impressive pillared porch.

Sheep fairs were held here from the time of Henry III until 1932. Stockbridge was on the main route for herds of stock being driven from Wales to Surrey and Kent, but with the coming of the railways these journeys declined.

This is still farming and racing country and St Peter's church has a roundel over the door leading to the choir vestry depicting one notable winner, *The Tetrarch*, always ridden by Steve Donaghue.

Parchment was made here at one time, no doubt helped by water from the river Test, and tanning was another local industry. A local clock-maker named Eack was

A quiet corner of Stockbridge

renowned for producing grandfather clocks with a painted face depicting vessels in full sail.

Stockbridge is built upon an artificial causeway thought to have been laid during Roman times to enable the main channel of the Test to be bridged. During the 10th century a frontier stronghold garrisoned by the Saxons was built on the causeway to defend Wessex against the Danes and it later became the main road between Old Sarum and Winchester.

⌘ SWAY

Estate agents describe Sway as a village in the heart of the New Forest. In fact it sprawls untidily on the southern edge of the forest.

For centuries a poor living was scraped from smallholding, farming and seasonal forest work. Smuggling and poaching were rife and in about 1777 the vicar of Boldre, whose parish then included Sway, described his parishioners as 'little better than bandits'.

The opening of the Brockenhurst to Christchurch section of the London & South Western Railway in 1888 changed the village in more ways than one. Prosperity was increased as businessmen moved in. They built houses, providing more local employment for labourers, craftsmen and domestic servants. Also two local roads were renamed Manchester Road and Brighton Road as a reminder of the railway gangs from those towns.

Sway has grown round the church, railway station and school and has not expanded so much as filling in. It is fortunately limited on two sides by the boundaries of the forest. There are no ancient buildings in the village, though there are a few cob cottages. A local landmark is Peterson's Tower, designed by Andrew Peterson on his retirement from India. It is 218 feet high and built of mass concrete by unskilled labourers who were paid five shillings a day. It was finished in 1885 and still stands straight and true.

Local myths associate Sway with docks and treacle mines! Ironic references to these among the older generation can be heard today. The origin of these myths is not known. However, it is interesting to note that there is a house called 'Switchells' built on the site of Switchells coppice and according to Chambers Dictionary the definition of 'switchel' is treacle-beer.

⌘ THRUXTON

Lying just to the north of the busy A303, Thruxton is a name familiar to those interested in gliding or car and motor-cycle racing. These events are held at the former Second World War airfield situated just to the west of the village and where there is also a busy little industrial estate.

Unlike the racing circuit, the village proper can hardly be seen from the main road. The centre of the village was declared a conservation area in 1985. There are many listed buildings, including cob boundary walls traditionally capped with thatch or tile. The village green, the seasonal stream and the surrounding houses, epitomise the idea of the English village.

Standing boldly in the centre of the village is the chapel of this former Wesleyan stronghold. It was built in 1875 and opinions differ as to its architectural merits. After the First World War it became the village Memorial Hall. It still hosts the full gamut of community activities.

The church of St Peter and St Paul dates back to the 13th century but much of what we see today is a result of 19th century rebuilding and recent restoration. Inside are a few treasures. Of particular note is a magnificent brass portrait of Sir John de Lisle, lord of the manor, who died in 1407.

Beyond the village there is evidence of Bronze and Iron Age occupation and traces of two Roman buildings have been discovered, the more important at Mullenspond. This was possibly a temple dedicated to Bacchus who is depicted on the mosaic pavement found under the rubble in 1823. In 1899 the owner of the site presented the mosaic and the terracotta candelabrum found at the same time, to the British Museum, where they can still be viewed.

Today it is wildlife found at Mullenspond which is of particular interest and fiercely protected. The present pond was created during the Second World War when gravel was excavated to lay the runways at the airfield. It naturalised quickly to become an outstanding feature of the locality and many villagers monitor the impressive variety of birds who use it as a home, or as a temporary stop.

⌘ TITCHFIELD

Lying at the heart of the growing 'metropolis' of south Hampshire, Titchfield still maintains much of its village charm.

The imposing ruins of Titchfield Abbey (taken by kind permission of English Heritage)

The highlight of the year in Titchfield is the annual bonfire carnival held on the last Monday of October. The carnival procession, the largest in Hampshire, winds its way round the village, with many village families entering floats; houses and business premises being decorated; Cole's funfair in attendance; and a large bonfire on the recreation ground. The origins of the carnival are shrouded in mystery, many believing it to date from the 15th century when the Earl of Southampton ordered the damming of the Meon estuary, thus effectively ending Titchfield's life as a port.

Titchfield Abbey, to the north of the village, became home to the Earls of Southampton after the Dissolution of the Monasteries and it is widely believed that William Shakespeare was a regular visitor.

A prominent feature of the village church of St Peter, which stands next to the river at the end of a narrow street leading from the village square, is the tomb of the Earls of Southampton.

Titchfield was once at the heart of a flourishing strawberry growing area, and although neighbouring Locksheath has seen its fields covered by housing estates, the farms surrounding Titchfield are still noted for today's Pick Your Own fruit trade. Titchfield was early to this business in the 1960s when local farmer Steve Harris was one of the first to open his fields to the public.

⌘ TWYFORD

Twyford, four miles south of Winchester, gets its name from the two fords across the river Itchen, world famous for its trout fishing. Today the village is bisected by the busy B3335 and the villagers would welcome two crossing places. However, the installation of traffic lights in the centre of the village has eased the crossing problem.

The present church of St Mary was rebuilt in 1878, but it incorporates the 12th century nave arcades and the font. A window in the north wall dates back to 1520. Under the tower are twelve stones in a circle. These, combined with a well and an ancient yew tree, are said to provide the circle, wood and water needed for Druidic worship. The yew tree was mentioned in the Domesday Book.

The whole village is full of history. A Roman villa was unearthed, at the top of Roman Road, in 1891. The Dolphin Inn is reputedly an 18th century coaching inn on the London to Southampton route. Twyford House also dates back to the early 18th century. It belonged to the Shipley family. Bishop Jonathan Shipley, Bishop of St Asaph, invited his friend Benjamin Franklin, the American statesman, to stay in 1771 and it was there that he wrote part of his memoirs.

Brambridge House stands on the edge of the village. The original house burned down in 1872, but the avenue of limes leading to the house was planted in the reign of Charles II. Brambridge House was the family home of Maria Smythe who, as the

Twyford

widowed Mrs Fitzherbert, contracted a morganatic marriage with the Prince Regent in December 1785.

The village has memories of various wars. The barn at Manor Farm was used to quarter troops during the Civil War. Army Row was built to house veterans of Waterloo. In the First World War troops were encamped on Hazeley Down, and in the Second World War Canadian soldiers were billeted in the village.

The only surviving custom is the Bell Ringers' Feast. Legend has it that William Davis was returning home on horseback over the downs when the mist came down. The bells of Twyford church warned him that he was on the edge of a deep chalk pit. In his will he left a guinea to the bell ringers so long as they rang a peal morning and evening on 7th October. The bells are rung accordingly and the bell ringers enjoy supper together afterwards.

The footpaths by the Itchen Navigation Canal and others leading up over the chalk downs reveal a wealth of plants, birds and insects and contribute to the pleasure of living in Twyford.

⌘ UPPER CLATFORD

Upper Clatford lies one and a quarter miles south of Andover. It is a most delightful village with a beautiful church and the river Anton flowing through the valley.

It was probably during the reign of Henry I (1100-1135) that the church of All Saints was first built. Its massive columns and round arches are typical of the first half of the 12th century. The church was partly rebuilt in the 16th century and the building transformed into an 'auditory church' in the 17th century.

The fine house known as Red Rice stands in the parish of Upper Clatford, having been built by General Webb in about 1740. General Webb was one of the Duke of Marlborough's subordinates, and it is said that the trees in the park surrounding the house represent the troop line-up at the battle of Malplaquet in 1709.

Bury Hill hill fort has no known history, unlike its famous neighbour Danebury Ring four miles away. Some exploration was carried out in the 1930s but did not bring forth much information.

A famous feature of Anna Valley (also part of the parish) was the well-known firm of Taskers which for more than 160 years provided employment for many local people. Founded in 1873 by three brothers, the foundry manufactured cottage pumps, agricultural machinery, steam engines, iron bridges (one is still in use today in the village by Fishing Cottage) and, during the Second World War, aeroplane trailers large enough to carry complete aeroplanes for the RAF.

The Tasker brothers provided housing, a school, church and a workman's rest for the people of Anna Valley. The school house can still be seen, called the Lodge. It has become one of the many Listed properties in the parish, many being beautiful thatched cottages several hundred years old, including the post office and the village pub, the Crook and Shears.

⌘ UPTON GREY

Upton Grey is one of Hampshire's most attractive villages, a pond at the junction of the village street and the Weston Patrick road, being a well known feature.

Known in Saxon times as Aoltone, and later as Upetone and Upetona, it was owned for 200 years by the De Grey family. In olden times the village was served by a baker, a blacksmith, a carpenter, a cordwainer, a maltster, a tailor and a wheelwright. Farming was the main industry.

St Mary's church dates back to Norman times, although there was a church on the site in Saxon times. The vicar now serves five parishes. There are also some fine old houses, one or two being 16th century and thatched. One is said to house the ghost of a monk, seen by various people over its 400 years.

The Pond House once housed the tailor, whose lamp lit up the pond. In those days it froze over in winter so the locals would skate on it by the light of the tailor's lamp. In another old house it is said that the men of the adjoining cottages met over a fence in their respective cellars for a glass of beer!

St Mary's church, Upton Grey, dates back to Norman times

The main village events revolve round the church and the village hall, such as the annual fete, cheese and wine parties and jumble sales. Happily the village still has its Flower Show on the second Saturday in August and the WI holds an annual party for pensioners each December. All these events bring together the long established and the new residents.

⌘ WALTHAM CHASE

A chase (or chace) was a piece of land reserved by the Crown for a local lord for hunting. After the Bishop's Palace had been built at Waltham in the 12th century, Waltham Chase was used as a hunting ground by successive bishops. The chase began at Waltham Park and ran to the south and east, stretching as far as the Bere Forest at Soberton, covering a much larger area than the present village.

The deer with which the Chase had been stocked were a nuisance to the labouring tenants whose crops they ate, but it was not until the 18th century that the Waltham Blacks appeared. They were young men who blacked their faces, disguised themselves and stole the bishop's deer. Further, they went on to rob stagecoaches and were much feared by travellers.

In 1722 Parliament, having been urged to do so by Bishop Trimmell, passed a

Black Act which listed hundreds of offences, many punishable by death. A gibbet was erected by the roadside hedge of what is now the Triangle Recreation Ground. Although scholars believe the Black Act was not called into use, the gibbet was used more than once. However in 1742 when Bishop Hoadley was asked to restock the Chase with deer, he refused, saying it had done enough harm already.

Waltham Chase village was enclosed in 1855, and, following enclosures, common wasteland was sold for seven shillings an acre. Market gardening became important and there were many smallholders. Strawberry growing was an important industry by the turn of the century, until the Second World War. Many growers took their fruit by horse and van to Botley station where they queued up for their turn to unload. The growers' carriage charges helped the railway and the service provided by the railway helped the growers. Much of the fruit was sent to London hotels.

⌘ WARSASH

Warsash is situated on the eastern bank of the river Hamble, near the entrance of the river into Southampton Water, and opposite the village of Hamble. The parish is known as Hook-with-Warsash because of the links with the nearby village of Hook.

Warsash sits on the eastern bank of the river Hamble

By the cross roads in the centre of the village is the clock tower, which was built as a water tower to supply Warsash House and estate with water. King Edward VII used to visit Warsash House when he was Prince of Wales. The house was pulled down and modern houses built just before the Second World War, but the water tower and model farmhouse remain. The clock on the tower struck ship's bell time until an electric clock was installed in 1945.

Shipbuilding and fishing were very important occupations – crabs, lobsters and shellfish provided the living for several families. Crab teas were provided near the shore and became famous locally. The Rising Sun (where teas were once served) is still a very popular public house.

The land in this area is very stony and is ideal for growing strawberries. Twenty years ago, on a fine summer's day the smell of strawberries was all pervading. The trade has been important to the area for many years, and you will still find strawberries being sold at the side of the road in season.

The College of Maritime Studies, situated where the old coastguard station used to be, has trained countless Merchant Navy seamen from all over the world. It is possible to steer one of the world's largest oil tankers and bring it into port and never leave the college buildings, thanks to modern technology!

Very near here, a century or more ago, salt was collected from the salterns after the sea water had evaporated. Wooden posts can still be seen at low tide marking this area.

A ferry runs regularly across the river Hamble to Hamble village. Some people travel to work that way, and it is very popular with holidaymakers.

⌘ WELLOW

Wellow covers a large area, divided by the river Blackwater into two parts known as East and West Wellow.

The church, St Margaret's, was built in 1216, and stands away from the village. It is thought that at one time it was probably in the middle of the village, before the evacuation of people due to the plague in 1665. The church is well known and is visited by many people, especially nurses, from all parts of the world, who come to see the grave of Florence Nightingale. The tomb bears a very simple inscription, 'F.N. 1820–1910', in accordance with her wishes.

Florence Nightingale lived at Embley Park during her childhood. The large brick house is now a public school for boys. The park and gardens contain many varieties of rhododendrons and azaleas. The farmland around it has changed somewhat in the last few years, as it has been planted with vines by Wellow Vineyards.

Connecting part of the Embley estate was a carriage driveway over a bridge on a roadway beneath. This was known as Sounding Arch, a very substantial construction of stonework. It was in a deep cutting and the actual archway was

St Margaret's church, in Wellow, was built in 1216

quite long, hence the name because noises echoed – horses' hooves, shouting, and later car horns. Stories were told of ghostly coaches passing over, past the iron railings on the top, at midnight on New Year or Christmas nights. The Sounding Arch was demolished, as road widening became necessary. A seat was made from some of the stone, and now marks the spot where once it stood. The roads and lanes about the village are still pleasant. One has a ford with a footbridge; this is Rix's Ford, and is a lovely quiet spot. In flood many cars get stuck, and it is not unusual for the local farmer to be called to the rescue with his tractor.

⌘ WEST MEON

Like many Hampshire villages, West Meon suffers the disadvantage of a surfeit of traffic. However, for its 700 inhabitants there are many advantages and the village enjoys a strong sense of community. The knapped flint church of St John built in 1846 has a fine set of eight bells. The river Meon runs through an area of outstanding natural beauty, and timbered and thatched houses add to the village's rural charm.

Mr Gardiner was the verger at St John's church. He mended shoes in the house now known as Warnford Corner. He was very strict and in the days when everybody went to church, including the children, he would rap the boys with his long staff if they misbehaved themselves. The boys of the village had their revenge. Late in life he married a widow at St John's and dressed in his best smock for the occasion. As he was returning from church with his bride all the boys of the village hid behind the wall and pelted them with clods of earth.

Opposite Warnford Corner is a house called Rose Cottage, which has had its staircase in three different places. Many, many years ago an old gentleman died there and the staircase then was so narrow that the coffin had to be lowered out of a bedroom window to the waiting bearers below. In another cottage in the village there is a 'coffin door' on the staircase to allow a coffin to be manoeuvred round the narrow, twisting stairs.

⌘ WHERWELL

Wherwell is in northern Hampshire and is situated on the river Test, a chalk stream

Cottages by the river in Wherwell

rising at Overton and flowing into Southampton Water at Redbridge. It is renowned for its fly fishing for trout, and occasionally salmon come this far up river to spawn.

When Winchester was the capital of England, Wherwell was a royal hunting lodge. In the 10th century Elfrida married King Edgar, who owned the manor, but after his death she murdered his son at Corfe Castle. In expiation of this crime she founded the abbey of Wherwell and ended her life in penance. Nothing remains today, but 'The Priory' was built on the same site. The present church of St Peter and Holy Cross was built on the site of one destroyed in 1858. A painting of the original church hangs there today.

An interesting charity recorded in the church is that in 1691 Philadelphia Whitehead, out of the yearly rent of the White Lion, made available twelve shillings a year forever, to be paid to twelve of the oldest parishioners. Today the brewers who now own the White Lion give a lump sum of money to be invested.

In the centre of the lawn at The Priory is a tree stump. The tree was blown down some years ago, and under the roots was found the body of a man covered by a hurdle. Legend says a great treasure is buried there, but anyone trying to recover it would pay the penalty of sudden death.

A weather vane depicting a cockatrice used to be fixed on the church spire but is now in Andover Museum. The story goes that many years ago, in a dungeon beneath the priory, a duck laid an egg, which was hatched by a toad and produced a cockatrice, a fearsome monster. A reward of four acres of land was offered to anyone who could slay the monster and various people lost their lives trying. A servant at the priory called Green obtained a large steel mirror, which was lowered into the dungeon. The cockatrice, seeing another of its kind, exhausted himself trying to kill the newcomer, whereupon the valiant Green descended into the dungeon and slew it with a spear. In Harewood Forest today there is a piece of land, exactly four acres, known as Green's Acres.

⌘ WHITCHURCH

Whitchurch is tucked in a fold of the hills where the river Test meanders. It had three old watermills, harnessing the water to run machinery for the making of silk cloth, and a fulling mill for the washing and thickening of woollen cloth.

The silk mill has recently been restored and works regularly weaving silk. A shop sells the finished product to the many visitors. The church of All Hallows was founded early and has additions of various periods, from the 13th to the 19th centuries. There is also a Methodist chapel, a modern Roman Catholic church and a very old Baptist chapel.

In the 16th century Whitchurch was one of the largest towns in Hampshire, on land with evidence of human habitation since Neolithic times. The White Hart Inn in the centre was an old coaching inn on the road to Salisbury. Then the railways came, bringing navvies to dig the Salisbury line. The men got thirsty so there were a large number of pubs, some of which are still functioning. Others are known now only by their names, such as the Pineapple. After the Second World War new housing estates were built and Whitchurch grew.

Although fishing on the Test may be a pastime for the rich, everyone can enjoy feeding the ducks from one or other of the bridges that cross the river in the area. The silk mill bridge or the town bridge are restful reminders that there is still wonderful country around Whitchurch.

⌘ WICKHAM

The lovely village of Wickham has a large square, said to be the second largest in the country. Shops surround the square, along with Georgian houses, and there are 16th century houses just around the corner.

Wickham was the birthplace of William of Wykeham, Bishop of Winchester and founder of Winchester College, in the 14th century.

The mound on which the church is built was used by Celts and Saxons for burial

Chesapeake Mill, Wickham

93

or religious rites. St Nicholas' was built by the Normans in 1120, but has been thoroughly altered since. Inside there is a large memorial to the Uvedale family, once lords of the manor.

In 1268 King Henry III granted a charter to the lord of the manor, Roger de Scures, to hold an annual fair. One has been held every year since – even during wartime.

The old Victory Hall, now converted into flats, beside the river Meon, was once a busy tannery where men from the village worked. Later it became a brewery, with heavy horses coming and going, pulling great drays loaded with barrels. After part of the building caught fire, it was rebuilt and there is still a plaque on the rear of the building saying 'Wickham Brewery rebuilt ANO DMI 1887 being the Jubilee Year of the Reign of H.M. Queen Victoria'. The brewery closed in 1910 and later the Victory Club was formed to commemorate victory in the First World War. It was used in the Second World War as home and refuge for many evacuees from Portsmouth and Southampton. There was an army headquarters in the Kings Head public house, Canadian soldiers at Rookesbury School, and army engineers took over part of a garage along the Fareham road. A great many of the engineers married local girls and settled here after the war.

⌘ WIELD

Wield comprises the two villages of Upper Wield and Lower Wield, the first being a 'green' village with the houses formally arranged round a green and the latter a 'street' village with the houses mainly along a single lane.

Upper Wield's most notable building is its 12th century church of St James. It still retains most of its Norman architecture and there are many vestiges of wall paintings which date from medieval times to Queen Anne's reign. Her royal coat of arms can be seen above the chancel arch. The church also contains a large memorial to Henry Wallop and his wife. This is not only a beautiful piece of alabaster carving but the inscription is a remarkable piece of snobbery which eulogises Henry's brother and appears to mention the deceased almost as an afterthought.

Looking from the green there is a charming scene of a group of thatched cottages with the church behind them. This is best seen in the early morning when the sun glints on the golden weathercock on the wooden church spire. Only one cottage is still thatched in the 'longstraw' or 'Hampshire' thatch, the others favouring the 'wheat reed' style which is more hard-wearing.

There is a tiny Primitive Methodist chapel, which speaks of dissension in the village 100 years ago. Religion caused great disruption in 1851 when William Budge, a Mormon, came from America looking for converts. They were baptised in Wield Wood pond and some emigrated to Utah. Between 1851 and 1861 the population of the village dropped by over a quarter. Some of these probably emigrated, while others went to work in factory towns hoping for better wages. The census of 1881 shows that 90 per cent of the population were engaged in agricultural or allied jobs. Today the percentage has dropped to less than 0.5 per cent.

The Yew Tree pub in Lower Wield is a popular place to eat. It is directly opposite one of the prettiest cricket fields in the county. This is a pleasant place to have a picnic on a summer Sunday. Straying from the match and walking through the village will reward you with the sight of some very attractive houses.

⌘ THE WORLDHAMS

Near Alton lies the village of East Worldham, situated dramatically on the top of an escarpment. The old road from Selborne to Binsted, now visible as two lanes, crosses the Kingsley to Alton road at East Worldham.

Philippa Chaucer, wife of the poet Geoffrey Chaucer, is said to be buried in the pretty church at East Worldham, and the coffin lid from her tomb, found in the chancel, is in a niche in the church. Chaucer's son was lord of the manor at Worldham and Keeper of Woolmer Forest. A wooded mound, visible from the main road and called King John's Hill, is the site of a royal hunting lodge.

Away from the main road and about a mile and a half through peaceful countryside is West Worldham. Here the little church, medieval in origin, adjoins a 16th century manor farmhouse. There is more history at Hartley Mauditt, still within the parish, where a few mounds in the soil mark a vanished village. St Leonard's church remains with its Norman architecture, delightfully situated beside a lake.

The Worldhams still cherish a strong sense of identity. Highlight of the year is the Fete and Flower Show. A Parish Walk takes place on Rogation Sunday.

⌘ THE WORTHYS

The four Worthys (Headbourne, King's, Abbot's and Martyr) are spread along the north bank of the river Itchen, north-east of Winchester. The villages and hamlets are listed in the Domesday Book, though not by their modern names. Kings Worthy was king's land, while the other villages belonged to the church.

In the mid 1920s excavations uncovered an abandoned grain-store pit of an Iron Age settlement. Further excavation eventually revealed a Roman villa. A stone head of a woman and a portrait head of a boy were authenticated by the British Museum as Roman. Other finds, including a fine table top, are in Winchester museum. During the Second World War when Nissen huts were being erected in the grounds of Worthy Park, a burial ground of Saxon origin was discovered.

In medieval times, the river Itchen played a large part in the life of the community. It was then navigable up to Alresford and was used for the transport of goods. There were a number of mills along the river, one of which remains now as a private dwelling at Abbots Worthy.

The railway came to the Worthys in about 1909, when the Didcot, Newbury and Southampton line was opened and a station built. The railway did not survive beyond 1960 and the A34 now runs along part of the track.

In the 1880s, Kings Worthy acquired a foundry, which came to be known as the Vulcan Iron Works. Its chief product was the hydraulic ram for raising water. The rams were exported all over the world where they gave sturdy service for many years in developing countries and put Kings Worthy on the world map. The business survived a disastrous fire in 1907, recorded by a Winchester photographer, whose pictures were reproduced as postcards.